Underlining copied from Duggan's copy
David Buck - St. James's, South Leigh
& Hinton Community.

The Agnostic's Tale

a fragment of autobiography

JOHN RAE

Text copyright © 2013 John Rae

ISBN-10: 1-909609-00-5

ISBN-13: 978-1-909609-00-6

All Rights Reserved

This edition first published in 2013 by:

Thistle Publishing

36 Great Smith Street

London

SW1P 3BU

"Is there a notion of hope (and of our responsibility to the future) that could be shared by believers and nonbelievers? What can it be based on now?"
Umberto Eco to Cardinal Martini, Archbishop of Milan in
Belief or Nonbelief, a Dialogue 1997.

"Life's but a walking shadow, a poor player,
That struts and frets his hour upon the stage,
And then is heard no more; it is a tale
Told by an idiot, full of sound and fury,
Signifying nothing."
Shakespeare, Macbeth.

A LETTER FROM FATHER TIMOTHY RADCLIFFE OP

I found my discussions with John Rae immensely stimulating. Besides, I felt that we did develop a friendship that meant much to both of us. I did my best to persuade John of the arguments for belief in God. In the end – and this is vastly over simplified - it came down to a question of whether the love that we experience has in it, as Christians believe, an element of the eternal and transcendent. When John came to draft his book, which he sent me for comment, he remained, I think, agnostic. He wrote that the atheists had the best arguments. I replied that was because of his definition of what was a valid argument, which was fundamentally a scientific argument, which can neither prove nor disprove God's existence. But he did say that he continue to be bothered by this question of the nature of love. And so when John invited me to come down and see him before I started my trip to Asia, it was to discuss this.

It was a deeply moving conversation. He said at the beginning that I must not imagine that I was going to make a convert of him at the last moment! And I knew that. But we continue to explore the nature of love, and whether it carried any intimations of immortality. I cannot say that we arrived at a conclusion. Perhaps the most important thing was the friendship and mutual affection with which we talked. When I said goodbye, I said that I would come to see him when I returned from Taiwan. He replied that he would not be alive.

So I said that I would therefore hope to see him in heaven and looked forward to pointing out that he had been wrong. He laughed! So my impression was that he remained a seeker, of immense intellectual ability and honesty.

With love,
Timothy.

DEDICATION

To our thirteen grand children in the hope that they will never be indifferent.

INTRODUCTION

I am not sure when I gave up trying to believe in the existence of God but it was about twenty-five years ago when I was in my late forties. At the time I was the head master of Westminster School and regularly took school services in Westminster Abbey. I saw nothing wrong in conducting Christian services when I was no longer a believer. It wasn't as if I had become an atheist; I had just ticked the box marked 'Don't know' and left it at that. Over the ensuing years I must have given thought to whether life had any meaning and whether death would be the end but I cannot remember worrying or even caring very much. I might have continued in this state of indifference for the rest of my life if it had not been for a chance meeting with the writing of Umberto Eco and it was his 'restless incredulity' that made me realise how equivocal and intellectually lethargic my agnosticism was.

It happened in January 2004, when we were staying with our daughter and her family in Wilton, Connecticut. The eastern seaboard of the United States was in grip of winter, with freezing temperatures and deep snow drifts. Each morning, when the snow ploughs had cleared the roads, my wife and daughter went shopping and on this occasion I asked them to drop me off at the vast warehouse-like bookstore that had a coffee shop attached. I had no book in mind but as I wandered along the shelves looking for something to read with my cappuccino, I spotted a small paperback entitled <u>Belief or Nonbelief: a dialogue.</u> The dialogue, which originally appeared in the form of letters in the Italian newspaper <u>Corriere della Sera</u>, was between Carlo Maria Martini, the Archbishop of Milan, and the philosopher, novelist and agnostic, Umberto Eco. I was intrigued and, taking the book with me to the coffee shop, I started to read.

As the argument went back and forth with each letter, I found myself excited by the debate I had opted out of. Does history's trajectory give human beings any cause to Hope that life is not just a tale told by an idiot, signifying nothing? Is there a notion of Hope (and of our responsibility to the future) that could be shared by believers and nonbelievers? Is it possible to sustain ethical values without a belief in God? The more I read, the more absorbed I was by the way the Roman Catholic Cardinal and the agnostic philosopher sought for the common ground without compromising their belief and nonbelief, but the crucial revelation for me was the nature of Eco's agnosticism, a restless incredulity that was far removed from my shoulder-shrugging 'Don't know'.

I don't think I knew there and then that I would no longer be content with my form of agnosticism but over the next few weeks I read the dialogue again several times and experienced the same excitement so that by the early spring I was impatient to take up the challenge it had thrown down. If I wanted to call myself an agnostic, I would have to find a way to shock or shake my agnosticism into something approaching restless incredulity. And the sooner the better. Like many people of my age – I was 73 in March 2004 – what I feared most was not death but senility and I remembered Marcus Aurelius's warning, 'Get on with the pursuit of truth before the mind starts to wander.'

I was pretty sure that pursuing the truth of what I believed or did not believe about the existence of God was not something that could be done by reading. The few modern books on theology I had dipped into, I had found almost impossible to understand. Modern theologians, I thought, use more and more obscure and impenetrable language to disguise the fact that they are less and less convinced of the reality of God's existence, but if I talked to believers face to face, as well as to atheists and fellow agnostics, I would be able to ask, 'What exactly do you mean by that?' So I conceived the idea of setting out on a journey to meet men and women who by the nature of the life they had chosen or the knowledge and insights I thought they possessed, seemed likely to be able to help me.

When I started, I did not know where my journey would end. I might still be an agnostic though hopefully of a much more rest-less kind, or I might discover that I was not an agnostic at all, just a believer who had lost his way or an atheist who refused to admit as much even to himself. I did not plan the whole journey in advance but after the first few stages, followed wherever my need for better understanding led me.

I was brought up as a Christian and have been close to Christian-ity all my adult life but I am not a theologian. Not long ago a man came up to me after a dinner and said: 'I shall always remember your sermon on the transfiguration'. As I had no idea what the transfigura-tion was, he had clearly mistaken me for someone else. I knew enough, however, to ask Christians to tell me exactly what they believed about the nature of God and the divinity of Christ. I did not want them to try to convert me (though two did), just to help me understand what their faith meant to them.

I was not sure what to do about the other world religions, whether to exclude them altogether or to risk the misunderstandings that would almost certainly follow a crash course in someone else's culture. In the end, I decided to look for an individual who had a profound understanding of the world's religions, not just an academic qualifica-tion in comparative religion. What I wanted to know was whether the other great world religions offered me an alternative way of under-standing the word God and, if they did, whether I would still call myself an agnostic.

This book is a record of my journey. It is a fragment of autobi-ography describing the year – roughly from the summer of 2004 to the summer of 2005 – when I set out to discover what I did or did not believe about God. To a professional theologian or philosopher I am sure it will appear superficial or muddled or both but it is not intended to be a book about theology or philosophy, just a personal account of what happened, of how people answered my questions and what I made of their answers.

I am very grateful to all the men and women who were willing to see me. Without exception they were welcoming and generous with their thoughts and time. In a number of cases, I asked the person concerned to check my account of our conversation because on the question of belief or nonbelief, it is easy to misrepresent people's views. For the record, the following checked my account and made suggestions that I incorporated in the final text: Martin Rees, Teresa Keswick, Richard Dawkins, Timothy Radcliffe, Don Cupitt, Robin Griffith-Jones, Simon Conway Morris, Karen Armstrong, Richard Holloway and Maria Boulding.

At my request, Timothy Radcliffe read the whole book and made a number of suggestions. I am very grateful to him for all his help. Any errors that remain and the conclusion I reach are my responsibility alone.

My greatest debt is to my wife, Daphne. Without her help I would never have met some of my most rewarding contacts. As a Roman Catholic, she must have had reservations about this project but she supported me throughout and for this I am especially grateful.

1

IN WHICH I VISIT T.H. HUXLEY'S GRANDSON AND QUESTION THE ASTRONOMER ROYAL

I have decided to start my journey in Cambridge. I am seeking support for my agnosticism from two of the best scientific minds in the University so that my arguments will be in better shape when I meet the atheists and the believers.

T.H. Huxley, the great Victorian biologist and friend of Darwin, coined the word agnostic to describe his own position. He was not prepared to accept without scientific evidence the existence of God, religious miracles and personal immortality, and he rejected the term atheist because the non-existence of God could not be proved scientifically. For my part, such has been my almost total lack of interest in the subject in recent years, I looked in the Oxford English Dictionary before I left home to see how the word agnostic was defined.

'One who holds that the existence of anything beyond and behind material phenomenon is unknown and (so far as can be judged) unknowable and especially that a First Cause and an unseen world are subjects of which we know nothing.'

No mention of God but he lurks rather coyly behind the words First Cause. I think this definition of what it means to be an agnostic is the same as mine though I could not have expressed it in such a carefully crafted way. For me, the one mystery that matters is why anything exists at all and the answer to that it will always be unknowable. To strengthen my resolve I have written on the corner of my notebook a quotation from Charles Darwin: 'The mystery of the beginning of all things is insoluble by us and I for one must be content to remain an agnostic.'

Sir Andrew Huxley is T.H. Huxley's grandson and Aldous Huxley's half-brother. He lives outside Cambridge in the village of Grantchester and I arrive in time for tea. The white house set in a large garden that backs onto open fields was built in 1928 but it has the air of one of those Russian properties to which, in Turgenev's novels and Chechov's plays, Moscovite families move during the summer months. While Andrew is putting the kettle on, I walk through the living room, which has a copy of John Collier's famous portrait of T.H. Huxley above the fireplace, and out into the garden where my Russian fantasy is re-enforced by the presence of a silver birch tree moving slowly in the breeze. With a little more imagination I could see Bazarov, Turgenev's nihilist, striding towards me over the flowerbeds.

A small round table covered with a cloth and laid for tea with drop scones and chocolate cake, has been placed in the centre of the lawn as though to ensure that our conversation will not be overheard. We have known one another off and on for several years because Andrew, as the Master of Trinity College, was a governor ex-officio of Westminster School. He won the Nobel Prize for Physiology in 1963. If he explained the nature of his work in physiology and experimental biophysics, I doubt whether I would understand a word but his reason for being an agnostic is straightforward. Why anything exists at all cannot be known. Like his grandfather, he believes that the existence of God can neither be proved nor disproved. The old arguments for God's existence have long ago been shown to be flawed. The idea of attributing the diversity of life on earth to God's creative design was discredited once and for all by Darwin's theory of natural selection.

There is no hint of scientific triumphalism in his attitude to religious beliefs, on the contrary he seems keen to point out that there are problems, such as the nature of human consciousness, that science might never solve, and to emphasise that he is an agnostic about a number of questions that interest theologians as well as biologists such as whether human beings have free will,

What does surprise me is to hear that his agnosticism also embraces the paranormal. Trinity College has received a bequest to fund research into the paranormal and Andrew has taken an interest. I remember reading that his other half-brother, the biologist Julian Huxley, also took an interest in the paranormal but decided most of it was trickery and mumbo jumbo after attending a séance at which the medium claimed to be in contact with Saint Teresa but when questioned was unable to say whether this was Saint Teresa of Avila or of Lisieux.

Andrew, too, is cautious. He thinks there might be something in thought transference and he is impressed by the evidence of children in India and Sri Lanka who have taken on the personality of someone who has recently suffered a violent death. I suspect the latter is trickery, too, but do not say so. I don't want my journey to be sidetracked by the paranormal.

Andrew has invited me to dine with him in College and I spend a pleasant evening at the top table in Trinity which is full, even in the middle of the university's long summer vacation. I am staying the night in one of the college guest rooms, the so-called Judges Room on the ground floor in a corner of Great Court, and when I have said goodnight to Andrew, I let myself into the room with a heavy iron key. There is no one else around in this part of the college except for the Judges of Assize who for four hundred years have slept here and whose portraits hang on the walls.

I can think of more congenial companions particularly as the light from the bedside lamp is so weak the far corners of this large room are in shadow but I read for a while unconcerned by the thought of the room's former occupants. When I turn off the light, however, I feel a strange flesh-creeping sensation as though a band of cold air is moving over my body. It is of course just a psychosomatic reaction to my gloomy surroundings and the talk of the paranormal, fuelled perhaps by the excellent port wine and stilton cheese. I tell myself that I am a rational man who does not believe in the supernatural but I turn the light on just to check that I am alone. Then I take up my book, it is Siegfried Sassoon's <u>Memoirs of an Infantry Officer</u>, and read. In the morning I laugh at childish fears; they are a timely reminder of how easily the illusion of an unseen world can be created by the imagination.

The present Master of Trinity College is Sir Martin Rees, the Astronomer Royal of Great Britain and a leading cosmologist. I want to talk with him because when I ask myself why anything exists at all, it is the vast universe I am thinking of, not how it came into being but why. That the answer to this question will always be unknowable is the foundation of my agnosticism and I want to be reassured that one of the world's authorities on the universe, when faced with that question, is agnostic too. I have reason to believe he is. When I wrote asking if he would help me on my journey, he replied, 'I am probably myself, in a state of mind similar to yours.'

We meet in his study at the Master's Lodge. Like Andrew Huxley, he has the eminent scientist's gift of speaking in plain English but while I understand what he is saying, I find it difficult to grasp the unimaginable measurements of space and time he is describing:

'Our universe extends millions of times beyond the remotest stars we can see, out to galaxies so far away that their light has taken ten billion years to reach us.'

To Martin Rees, the cosmologist, our earth is just a tiny speck in a vast universe which may itself be only one of many universes, and that speck will not live for ever. In about six billion years the sun will die and our earth with it; all life on earth will be vaporized, wiped out leaving no trace.

'Then Macbeth was right.' I suggest, 'life is a tale told by an idiot, full of sound and fury, signifying nothing.'

Martin Rees disagrees. On that time scale, it is possible that human beings will have colonised other planets in the universe and that life will continue there. But even if all life is extinguished, that does not mean that our lives have no significance. He does not believe that life has a purpose beyond itself but that we have a purpose here and now to make progress in our understanding of the universe, in our organisation of society and in our stewardship of the planet; and as he talks about the remarkable advances that human beings have made and have still to make on the frontiers of science, I am reminded of the Epicurean idea that although we are mortal, we can achieve a kind of immortality by engaging in the eternal task of extending our knowledge of nature and the universe.

Even so, if the ultimate destiny of all human endeavour is going to be oblivion, has he never considered being an atheist.

'What God would I not believe in?' he replies.

He is sure that the only rational position is agnosticism. What he calls 'the pre-eminent mystery' of why anything exists at all will always be beyond the range of our thought and language but he sees no reason to believe in a personal God. His priority is those other mysteries about the universe that he believes science will eventually solve and he uses one of these, the remarkable combination of circumstances that makes our universe hospitable to life, to illustrate how science and religion interpret these mysteries in a different way. To scientists who are Christian believers, the remarkable combination of circumstances gives us more than a hint of a Divine Presence but Martin Rees believes there must be a scientific explanation that does not include God. If our universe is only one of many universes, he suggests, it would not be so surprising that it should be fine-tuned to be hospitable to life, though how the pre-requisites for life emerged over the thirteen billion years since the universe began remains cosmology's most daunting challenge.

Anxious to bring our conversation down to earth I ask whether he goes to church. As Master, he attends services in the college chapel but he also attends church services for their own sake; he likes the ritual and the sense of community, aspects of our society that are disappearing. He is not wavering in his agnosticism; he describes himself as a practising but unbelieving Christian, 'a parasite on the church'. He would be sorry to see the Church of England fade away which he fears may happen if the Anglican clergy continue to be evasive about their beliefs. When he asks them what it is essential for a Christian to believe – is it the incarnation, the resurrection, life after death or none of these? – they do not seem to know. There is a note of frustration in his voice as though he is impatient with the church for not putting up a better fight against the advance of science.

Does he think there can be constructive dialogue between religion and science? He shakes his head. 'Peaceful co-existence but not constructive dialogue'.

As he accompanies me downstairs to the front door that opens onto Great Court, he says, 'Of the world's religions, Buddhism is probably the best bet as long as you don't have to believe in re-incarnation.'

I thank him and walk out into the bright August sunshine. Trinity's Great Court, with its fine lawns, renaissance fountain and early seventeenth century buildings is surely one of the most beautiful quadrangles in the world. It was the creation of Thomas Neville, a Master of the college much favoured by Elizabeth and James I, and a powerful defender of the Calvinist doctrine of predestination that divided humanity into the Damned and the Elect.

I walk across to the chapel and, finding the interior cool and deserted, sit in one of the stalls to write up my notes of the meeting. I am pleased with the result of my visit to Cambridge. I am more confident now that I am right to be an agnostic and I am ready to take on the believers and the atheists but something that Martin Rees said nags in my mind.

It is ridiculous for me to worry about an event that will occur six billion years in the future but I cannot help thinking about the time when the sun will die and the earth with it and the fact that there will be no trace, no memory anywhere in the universe that life on earth ever existed. I wish he had not told me that, though I expect it is common knowledge. The thought that the human adventure is going to end in oblivion may tilt my agnosticism, if not towards atheism, then at least towards Pessimism rather than Hope. I am about to leave the chapel when I remember something else that Martin Rees said about galaxies so far away that their light has taken ten billion years to reach us. Does that mean that the light that will arrive on earth when all life has been extinguished and the human adventure is over forever, is already on its way towards us?

I return to the Master's Lodge and, with apologies for troubling him again, put the question to Martin Rees. Yes, the light is already on its way towards us. 'I would just mention,' he adds, 'that I see no reason to envisage humans as being any more than an intermediate, perhaps relatively early, stage in the emergence of cosmic complexity – certainly not the culmination. Any creatures, on earth or far beyond, who witness the sun's death-throes six billion years hence – and who receive the light now setting out from distant galaxies – will be as different from us as we are from protozoa.'

Will it make any sense then, I wonder, to talk about the Damned and the Elect?

2

IN WHICH I TALK WITH THE PRIORESS OF A CARMELITE MONASTERY

Quidenham Hall in Norfolk has been a Carmelite Monastery since 1948. The women's branch of this Roman Catholic religious order owes its character to Saint Teresa of Avila, the great reforming nun of the 16th century. If a medium ever did succeed in contacting this remarkable woman, he would be left in no doubt which St. Teresa he was talking to. Saint Teresa of Avila was a mystic and a contemplative who nevertheless possessed the energy and determination to transform the corrupt Spanish monasteries into standard-bearers of the Counter Reformation. It is said that the gentle poet, St. John of the Cross, whom she recruited to her cause, never knew what hit him when he signed up with this strong-willed woman. In the monastery of which she was Mother Superior, she returned to the early Carmelite ideals of prayer, poverty and enclosure and these still dictate the character of the Carmelite life.

In preparation for my meeting with the Prioress of a 21st century Carmelite monastery, I have read some passages from Saint Teresa's writing, especially her letters, and found that they are full of genuine humility and insights into human nature. The present prioress at Quidenham is Sister Teresa Keswick. When I telephoned to make an appointment, she asked if I ate smoked salmon; it would be my good fortune to arrive on a day when the nuns were enjoying this rare treat, a gift from her brother who is a keen fisherman.

The nearest station is Diss and from here it is a twenty-minute taxi ride to the monastery. The young man who is driving me has just set up a business on his own with two cars and says that there is a lot of competition for customers in this small market town.

He seems ambitious and levelheaded but when he hears why I am going to the monastery, he says, 'You don't want to know what I believe,' so I ask him. 'I believe we are all descended from aliens,' he replies and naturally I think he is joking. But he is serious. The evidence he cites is 'all those stories in the bible about lights in the sky.'

I let the matter drop, pretending to be interested in the flat East Anglian countryside. First ghosts and now aliens; if I was a credulous person, I would suspect a plot to throw me off the scent. When we arrive at Quidenham, the driver gives me one of his cards. 'They might need a taxi from time to time,' he says. I don't think he knows this is an enclosed community.

Sister Teresa greets me at the front door but then has to go by a different route to the room where we will talk. She has to approach the room from the monastery and I from the outside world. We sit on either side of a low wooden bench that divides the room from wall to wall. She cannot cross to my side or I to hers. She is in her mid-fifties, a sturdily built woman in her dark brown habit, with pleasant, open features and an air of authority. She comes from a family with commercial interests in the Far East.

Her father was a lowland Scottish Protestant, her mother a Roman Catholic. She says she was an atheist until the age of twelve when at a convent school in Paris she was present at a retreat preached by a priest who knew how to talk to the young about faith. Up to then she thought of religion as a 'one of those horrible things you did not have to do when you were grown-up.' In her early thirties, she realised that her life was going nowhere and that she was becoming, in her own words, 'a very nasty person'. It was then that she felt drawn towards the Carmelite life of prayer and poverty and she entered the monastery at Quidenham twenty-one years ago.

We talk for two and a half hours with a break for lunch and Nones, the early afternoon office which I am allowed to attend. I have not come to the monastery to hear intellectual arguments for the existence of God. I want to know what God means to someone who has committed her life to a close relationship with Him and to discover how important to her are the fundamentals of Christian belief such as the resurrection and hope of life after death.

She spent five years as a novice before making her Final Profession. Her novice mistress set a very good example and it was largely thanks to her guidance that Sister Teresa experienced what she calls, 'a distinct improvement in my character.' This is not a boast. She wants me to know that her 'change of heart' is the sort of miracle she believes in.

When I ask about life after death, she does not appear to be unduly worried. 'My natural reaction is that death is the end,' she says, 'but I choose to believe the Church's teaching'. She is adamant that she does not strive to be a better person in order to guarantee a place in heaven but then she adds, 'Perhaps God's love will find a way to enable what is best in each of us to survive.'

In a not dissimilar way she is able to hold two complementary ideas about the resurrection: it was a real event because there is no other way to explain the extraordinary impact on history of the risen Christ, yet at the same time it is a metaphor for God's victory, a shout of triumph, 'We've won!' I am reminded of the hymn that Westminster pupils enjoyed singing not because they were victorious Christians but because it had a rousing tune and robust words:

'T'is finished, all is finished,
The fight with death and sin;
Then open wide the golden gates
And let the victors in.'

If I put a contemporary spin on those words, I think I may come close to what Sister Teresa means when she talks about the resurrection as a shout of triumph. She means triumph over whatever is most selfish and destructive in our human nature; it is the fight with sin rather than with death that is important to her since we cannot escape, alter or interrupt death; but with our God-given free will we can at the very least attempt to live and act in a way that a well-informed conscience indicates. If I am right and she is saying that the resurrection represents the exciting possibility that the teaching and example of Jesus may prove stronger in the end that the self-interest and egoism that appear to be our genetic inheritance, I can go along with that, but I do not have to believe in the existence of God to admire the ethics of Jesus' sermon on the mount.

We break for lunch and Sister Teresa brings me a tray loaded with good things before going back into the monastery. Sitting alone, I enjoy the smoked salmon sent by her brother, bread rolls baked in the monastery and strong cheddar cheese. Then at a quarter to two, I make my way to the chapel to attend Nones. A young nun smiles as she hands me a copy of the Divine Office but says nothing. According to Sister Teresa, Carmelite nuns are not supposed to stare at strangers, though they are expected to be welcoming. I sit on one side of the sanctuary looking across the altar to where the nuns are silently assembling. There are twenty altogether with two wearing the white headdress of novices. High above the organ, two elderly nuns follow the service from behind a grill, which is there for reasons of safety rather than exclusion.

As an agnostic, I do not feel uncomfortable in a religious service even one as private as this. The nuns chant the psalms in monotone and I try to follow the words but although the young nun has marked the pages with coloured ribbons, I am soon lost. The pleasure is listening. Like Martin Rees, I am a parasite on religion; I like to participate from time to time without any obligation. At the end of the service, a metal gate is drawn across the opening between the nuns' pews and the altar.

When we resume our conversation, I ask Sister Teresa more about her beliefs.

'Do you believe in Hell?'

'No.'

'What about the existence of the soul?'

'That is much more technical than I can handle.'

When I asked Andrew Huxley the same question, he said he was agnostic on the subject; it was possible that the soul, while having no independent existence, was an epiphenomenon, a side effect of something else going on in the brain in a purely mechanical sense. And that was much more technical than I could handle.

I return to the principal purpose of my visit. In what sense is her God real to her? 'The thing to go for is God the Father, as shown to us by Jesus his son,' she replies. She did not always have a good relationship with her own father but she knows what a good relationship ought to be. The key to her relationship with God the Father is prayer and once again it is clear that it is her personal experience that persuades her of God's existence not sophisticated arguments about who designed the universe and set it in motion.

Two hours each day, one at 6.30 in the morning and one in the evening, are set aside for private prayer. 'For one hour you are alone with God.' I ask her who she is talking to during that hour and she replies, 'It feels as though you are talking to yourself much of the time and it is easy to slip into a Mills and Boon daydream.'

Saint Teresa of Avila had the same difficulty concentrating during the hour of prayer. 'For myself,' she wrote, 'very often I was more occupied with the wish to see the end of the hour. I used actually to watch the sand-glass.'

Sister Teresa uses scripture, the Saint's writing or the poems of George Herbert to draw her thoughts back from daydreams to God. She may share with Him the frustrations she sometimes feels as Prioress of this small community, for instance her impatience with a nun who cannot understand the loneliness of one of the older sisters who is confined to her cell, and by doing so feels she is given, not easy answers to life's frustrations but a greater understanding of what it means to love God and to love your neighbour. 'It may all be wishful thinking,' she concludes disarmingly but everything about her suggests that she does not believe that for a moment.

I could dismiss her prayer as some sort of do it yourself therapy but she tells me about it in such an honest and unpretentious way I am bound to believe that God is real for her and that is all that matters. I do not doubt the depth and sincerity of her belief, all the more convincing because it does not need the promise of heaven or the threat of hell or Thomas Aquinas's Five Ways to prove that God exists but it is a belief I do not share.

The taxi driver who believes that the origin of life on this planet was a visit by aliens long ago, will soon arrive to take me back to the railway station at Diss, so I ask Sister Teresa if she has any objection to my identifying her in my account of our meeting. On the contrary, she says, she would wish me to do so. 'The more personal your book is, the more interesting it will be.'

It is late September and sitting outside waiting for the taxi I feel the first chill of autumn. I shall soon have to put my agnosticism to a different test but it is so quiet and peaceful here I am reluctant to think ahead to meetings I have arranged with atheists. It is inconceivable that I would ever have considered entering a religious order, my father like Sister Teresa's would have had a heart attack, but then I remember that my best man was a Franciscan friar from Cerne Abbas and that although we were good friends I never asked him why he chose that way of life. I am sure there are down-to-earth explanations for the choice that Brother Peter and Sister Teresa made but their motivation was strong enough to carry them through their novice years, past the moment when they could have decided to leave and on into the full life of a Franciscan friar and a Carmelite nun. That suggests to me that down-to-earth explanations may not be the whole story but I find it hard to believe that the missing factor is a supernatural agency which they call God.

3

IN WHICH I ATTEND A MEETING
AT CONWAY HALL AND MEET
A PROMINENT ATHEIST

Many people who do not believe in God would not wish to be called atheists. Atheism has a bad name. It is associated in people's mind with other unattractive '-isms' such as anarchism, communism and fascism as though one bad thing was bound to lead to another and however unjust this guilt by association, it strengthens the popular prejudice. Not long ago the evidence of a defendant's bad character in a criminal trial was that he was 'an atheist and a wife beater.'

For the British and especially for the English, the word 'atheist' also has overtones of foreignness and bad form. The English attitude to religion was set four hundred years ago when Queen Elizabeth the First declared that she 'would not open windows into men's souls.' Go through the motions of religious observance and no questions will be asked. The truth of religion was something better left unexamined; what mattered was that religion provided the underpinning of good morals. This sensible hypocrisy still influences our public life with the result that most English people are uncomfortable with both excessive religious zeal and militant atheism. It is bad form to take your belief or non-belief too seriously.

I share some of this prejudice so I approach my first encounter with atheists determined to try to keep an open mind. I am attending a meeting at Conway Hall in London's Red Lion Square. The meeting has been organised by South Place Ethical Society, 'a free thought community' that formally rejected the existence of God in 1888. This is atheist territory.

The officials of the Society have been most helpful and seem to be genuinely anxious to encourage my project but at the meeting, the audience are in a less tolerant mood. They have come to hear a panel of speakers, including the journalist Polly Toynbee and the biologist Richard Dawkins, discuss the topic of free speech, and it is soon clear that as far as the audience is concerned, free speech means the freedom to mock religion. One speaker in particular feeds their frenzy. He is a cartoonist and speaks well on humour as a weapon against bigotry but when he shows slides of some of his cartoons, I am angered both by some of the cartoons and by the audience's reaction to them. One cartoon shows the Pieta, MichaelAngelo's sculpture of Mary holding in her arms the body of the crucified Christ, with a bubble issuing from Christ's lips containing the words, 'O shit, I've forgotten Mother's Day again.' The shrieks of laughter have an unpleasant, almost hysterical edge.

Richard Dawkins speaks last and I have the impression that despite his well-publicised atheism, he is embarrassed by the shrillness of the laughter. I slip out of the meeting before the end. Dawkins whom I will go and see because this audience has played too conveniently into the hands of my prejudice and I know there must be another form of atheism, one that can command my respect not my contempt.

A few days later I am in Oxford. It is early October, the start of the University term and the best time of the year, when the stuffy summer days are over and the tourists have gone. Richard Dawkins is the Charles Simonyi Professor of the Public understanding of Science and a fellow of New College. His reputation as a world famous biologist, an outspoken atheist and the author of best-selling books, notably The Selfish Gene, is rather daunting but he is no less friendly and welcoming than Sister Teresa.

We exchange views on that curious evening at Conway Hall before getting down to business. I am here to discover why he is an atheist and what distinguishes his atheism from my agnosticism. On the pre-eminent mystery of why anything exists at all, he is an agnostic but just as I am about to pounce, he makes it clear that this in no way modifies his atheism. He is an atheist because he rejects the idea that the solution to the pre-eminent mystery is some sort of intelligent super being. There is no evidence for the existence of God and – here he echoes Andrew Huxley's words – all the so-called proofs of God's existence were rendered worthless by Darwin. Evolution is blind in the sense that it is not guided by a forward-looking intelligence so there is no possibility that life is subject to outside direction or has a purpose beyond itself.

The difference between his atheism and my agnosticism is that although we agree that the reason why anything exists at all is unknowable, he wishes to add a rider to the effect that the reason cannot be God. I am not doing justice to the carefully thought out scientific argument that underpins his atheism but our exchange leads me to speculate on the following lines.

We are all born into a culture and grow up with the beliefs of that culture but at some point we have to confront the fundamental question of why anything exists at all. At that point we are all agnostic because the answer cannot be known. Some people do not see any reason to move from that position and so they remain agnostics. Others believe that behind the unknowable is God and so they swiftly reject agnosticism in favour of God's existence. Atheists like Dawkins, reject agnosticism for a different reason; they are convinced that God is a purely human invention and therefore can never be the reason why anything exists.

I am interested to know whether Dawkins thinks that the non-existence of God really is beyond dispute. He shows me a book written by one of his Christian critics in Oxford, which assumes that because you can't prove the non-existence of God, this somehow makes his existence and his non-existence equally probable. In effect, says Dawkins, the author assumes without argument that the evidence for and against the existence of God is finely balanced and if you want to gamble there is a fifty-fifty chance you will be right.

I suggest this sounds like a revised version of Blaise Pascal's famous wager that it is better to bet on God's existence because, 'if you win you win everything, if you lose you lose nothing.' But for Dawkins the evidence is overwhelmingly one sided and the only rational bet is to put all your money on the certainty that God does not exist. 'Merely to assert the unprovability of god's non-existence' he adds, 'does not, in itself put the hypothesis of his existence on an equal footing with the hypothesis of his non-existence'.

I ask about his work on the biology of selfishness and altruism and am interested to find that when we talk about the crisis in the Sudan, he cares about the suffering there in a way that I find it hard to do. On the other hand, we agree that if we saw a man in the street outside beating a child with a stick we would both run out to stop him. But Dawkins does not accept that human compassion is anything other than a product of evolution. According to Christians, compassion for other human beings and especially acts of striking selflessness testify to the presence of God as the supreme source of goodness, and it is one of their central criticisms of Dawkins' work that it excludes altogether the possibility of a role for the Divine. So I ask Dawkins how evolution accounts for this degree of human unselfishness that in the wild would quickly be eliminated by natural selection.

He gives me the proof of an article he has written for an American journal and I read it later sitting on a bench in the University Parks, a short walk from his house. The article, entitled <u>Atheists for Jesus</u>, is a <u>jeu d'esprit</u> but behind the light touch is a serious argument that answers my question.

Dawkins acknowledges that examples of what he calls 'human superniceness' or 'unDarwinian selflessness' do occur and that they represent something unprecedented in four billion years of evolution but he dismisses the idea that they require some supernatural explanation. Evolution has developed the human brain to a point where with foresight we can calculate the long term consequences of our actions and this is what enables us to divert selfish genes from their Darwinian goals.

It would be sensible, Dawkins suggests, for us to encourage this human superniceness in any way we can, a campaign in which atheists like himself would happily take the lead, even though the outstanding example and advocate of human superniceness was Jesus Christ. He argues that only by separating Jesus' teaching from 'the supernatural nonsense that he inevitably espoused as a man of his time', can we recognise how original and radical Jesus' ethic was. So atheists are for Jesus.

Many people who do not believe in the existence of God admire Jesus as a prophet and teacher but I do not think that anyone has linked the ethics of Jesus' teaching with the idea that it is only as a result of evolution that human beings are capable of following Jesus' example, that is to say, capable of rebelling against their selfish genes.

A man who wants to separate Jesus from 'the supernatural non-sense' that still clings to him and is adamant that blind evolution makes the idea of a Divine Presence in the Universe ridiculous is not likely to endear himself to the church and Dawkins has been attacked by churchmen for what they see as his intellectual arrogance and intolerance. In my meeting with him, I encounter neither of these qualities, and I cannot help contrasting his thoughtful and humane atheism with the shrieks of laughter in Conway Hall. He does not want to mock Christianity however much he enjoys provoking theologians and he has certainly made me think why, if I do not believe in the existence of God, I am not an atheist.

4

IN WHICH I ASK A SCIENTIST WHO IS A CHRISTIAN FOR PROOF OF GOD'S EXISTENCE

As an agnostic I am sceptical of the idea that modern science has room for an argument in favour of God's existence but if Andrew Huxley and Richard Dawkins say that the traditional arguments have been undermined once and for all by Darwin, I must at least consider the possibility that on this point alone the Darwinians may be wrong. If God has survived the theory of natural selection, I shall be interested to know where a scientist would say he could be found.

I am aware that looking for logical, intellectual arguments for God's existence is probably a wild goose chase, and that the only argument that counts will be found in personal experience or as Sister Teresa might have said if I had put the question to her directly, 'Where God is concerned, the proof of the pudding is in the eating.' Nevertheless, I am returning to Cambridge to meet a former professor of mathematical physics who has tried to reconcile his knowledge of modern science with his belief in the existence of God.

John Polkinghorne (it is an old Cornish name) is an ordained Anglican priest as well as a former Cambridge professor and President of Queens College. A prolific writer, he is one of the most widely read authors in the field of sciences and religion. In 2002 he was awarded the Templeton Prize for Progress in Religion, given each year 'to a living individual who has shown extraordinary originality in research or discoveries to advance understanding of God and spiritual realities.' The first recipient of the prize was Mother Teresa of Calcutta.

So far I have been fortunate in the warmth of the welcome I have received on my journey and John Polkinghorne, who looks like a Cornish farmer with his round face and ruddy cheeks, is no exception. He lives in a quiet suburban street out of the swing of the university town.

At the start of our conversation, he wishes to make one thing clear. He himself believes in God's existence because he encounters Him in prayer and in the Eucharist but if I am looking for some intellectually satisfying reasons for believing in the <u>possibility</u> that God exists, he is happy to oblige. He does not, I notice, use the word 'proof'. Nor does he mention Thomas Aquinas though his approach is similar to that of the great thirteenth century Dominican scholar. God's existence is not self-evident so it needs to be demonstrated by arguing from the effect back to the cause, in other words we have no direct knowledge of God but we can find hints of his Divine Presence in what we do know about the world around us.

The first of John Polkinghorne's intellectually satisfying reasons is the rational beauty of the cosmos, by which he means (I have to ask) the fact that on the very largest scale and the very smallest scale, the structure of the universe can be expressed in concise and elegant mathematical terms. I have no idea what these mathematical terms are but I understand him to be offering me an up to date version of the traditional argument that the orderly and complex design of the universe implies the existence of a designer. But Polkinghorne goes further than this. He thinks it cannot be pure chance that humans have the ability to uncover this mathematical structure and he is convinced that the individuals who made the crucial breakthroughs in our understanding were, whatever their religious beliefs, 'participating in an encounter with the Divine'.

He talks fast and there is such a vast gulf between his understanding of science and mathematics and mine that I sometimes feel that I am only grasping at the shirt-tails of an argument that flies by. It beggars belief, he continues, that it is just a happy accident or inexplicable good fortune that our universe should be fine-tuned for the development of conscious life. He knows that his former pupil, Martin Rees, will argue that if there are many universes our good fortune is not so extraordinary but Polkinghorne believes that the idea of a Divine Purpose behind our apparent good fortune is also an intellectually satisfying explanation.

We take a break and I have time to reflect. The first thing that comes to mind when I think about John Polkinghorne's arguments is von Clausewitz's advice on how to conduct a retreat after a lost battle. Unlike some of his fellow Christians who have thrown in the towel and declared that God is dead, John Polkinghorne continues to resist and, as von Clausewitz recommended, he offers 'bold courageous counterstrokes'.

He now suggests two more 'intimations of the Divine', not this time in the character of the physical fabric of the universe but in the way we think and feel and behave. It is, he says, of the highest significance that we live in a moral world and that our moral sense tells us that love and truth are better than hatred and lies. Evolution is a wholly inadequate explanation for this; our moral intuitions are 'whispers of God's presence' not examples of our ability to rebel against our selfish genes.

I am not convinced. There is no logical reason to argue that our sense of right and wrong points to the existence of God. I have doubts too about his next claim which is that God is behind our hope that life is not a tale told by an idiot, signifying nothing. Of course we hope but it does not follow that because we do, there really is something to hope for. On the other hand, hope that our lives might have some ultimate meaning has been such a universal human characteristic that I am reluctant to dismiss this argument altogether. Hope is where my journey started.

In one of his letters to Cardinal Martini, Umberto Eco wrote, 'Only by having a sense of history's trajectory can one love earthly reality and believe there is still room for Hope.' That was the sentence that caught my imagination and even though I now know the human adventure is going to end in oblivion, I still find Eco's 'room for Hope' appealing.

How does John Polkinghorne reconcile hope with the inevitable end of all life on this planet? He says his faith is not shaken by the prospect of what he calls 'cosmic futility'. If the human adventure is no more than a 'temporary flourishing' followed by oblivion, then 'Macbeth was right and it is indeed a tale told by an idiot' but he hopes for a human destiny beyond death, so the end of life on our planet presents no greater challenge to his belief in God than his own mortality. God's intentions, he adds, will not be frustrated by the end of the universe. He does not accept that the battle has been lost.

I cannot help admiring the ingenuity of his bold counterstrokes though I doubt whether they will delay the advance of secularism for long. He gives me a lift to the station and on the way reminds me that for him, God exists because he meets Him every day; the hints of God's presence he has been describing to me are intended to encourage a nonbeliever to take the possibility of God's existence seriously.

The implications of this do not strike me at first but on the way home when I ask myself whether he has succeeded in encouraging me to take the possibility of God's existence seriously, I realise that he never had a chance. My mind was firmly closed against the idea.

This is a fine time to discover that my open-mindedness is a lie. When I started my journey two months ago I thought I could be equally open to God on one hand and atheism on the other and that if I had a prejudice it was against atheism but now I have another prejudice to declare. I do not think I have ever taken seriously the possibility that God exists.

This requires some explanation. The deep-rootedness of my agnosticism is not something I am ashamed of. There were times when I genuinely thought of myself as a believer but I always knew that my interest in Christianity was more in the nature of an enquiry than a commitment. What happened twenty-five years ago was not that I became an agnostic but that after flirting with Christianity off and on over many years, I decided to settle for the single life.

Even if I had been open-minded, I would not have been persuaded by John Polkinghorne's case for taking the possibility of God's existence seriously. He claims that a Creator with a Divine Purpose is an 'intellectually satisfying explanation' for the fact that our universe is fine-tuned for the developments of conscious life. But belief in a Creator with a Divine Purpose is a leap of faith, and expression of hope, and cannot be an intellectually satisfying explanation for the way our material world is constructed.

I am not surprised that a distinguished mathematician and physicist who became an ordained priest should want to argue that belief in a Divine Creator is not incompatible with modern science but I am surprised that he chooses to do it this way. Discovering 'intimations of the Divine' in the universe leaves you open to the charge of planting evidence. Better surely to let science and religion go their separate ways. If you believe in a Divine Creator, science can never prove you wrong but neither can science provide the evidence to prove you right. I cannot match John Polkinghorne's knowledge of science and theology so I am puzzled that he does not see what to the layman seems so obvious. Science and religion are not at odds, they are just not connected.

5

IN WHICH I ATTEMPT TO TAKE SERIOUSLY THE POSSIBILITY THAT GOD EXISTS

I am not going to be persuaded to take the possibility of God's existence seriously by arguments based on the structure of the universe but my visit to Sister Teresa Keswick, Prioress of the Carmelite Monastery at Quidenham, suggests that I try a different approach. If I could find other men and women whose lives, like Sister Teresa's, have been transformed by their conviction that God exists, their faith and their example might help to overcome my prejudice. Many years ago I missed an opportunity of discussing this approach with one of the few people I have met whose life unambiguously declared the existence of God. Basil Hume was a Benedictine monk who became Cardinal Archbishop of Westminster. He asked me to chair the governing body of his choir school so we were often in contact; the opportunity was there but I never took it. Now I can read his talks and homilies but it is not the same.

I have no reason to believe that the people I am looking for will be well known; on the contrary, I shall be wary of celebrity saintliness. Nor have I any reason to think that members of Roman Catholic religious orders are more likely to be convincing witnesses to the existence of God than Protestants and lay people but I am going to begin this stage of my journey nevertheless by meeting a Jesuit priest and a Dominican friar.

Father Anthony Meredith lives in the Jesuit Residence attached to Farm Street Church in the heart of Mayfair, London's most expensive and fashionable district. The Jesuits have never been reluctant to rub shoulders with the rich and powerful or to be martyred for their faith. In the reception at the Residence is a recruiting poster that reads:

'Our Jesuit martyrs who have died for their faith and their people in many parts of the world show that Jesuits live under the banner of the Cross and the Cross is the sign that as followers of Christ we will be spared nothing.'

Father Anthony Meredith is a tall, distinguished looking man in his sixties with a scholarly manner that suggests the senior common-room rather than martyrdom, and I am not surprised to hear that he has been in Oxford for twenty years. He sometimes shared the top table at New College with Richard Dawkins and recalls that Dawkins, though an atheist, strongly opposed a suggestion that the Latin grace before dinner should be dropped or curtailed.

'What sort of agnostic are you?' Father Anthony asks. 'One who does not know whether God exists or one who believes there is an unknown god?'

I hesitate. The Jesuits have a reputation for clever argument and I do not want to be trapped. I reply that although I have at times been a Christian fellow traveller I have always been an agnostic at heart but I don't think my agnosticism falls into either of his categories. I am agnostic simply because I do not know why anything exists at all.

That is also Father Anthony's starting point but he is a cradle-Catholic and has never doubted that behind that pre-eminent mystery is God, and as I listen to him talking about his faith, I am amazed to find a Christian who still holds traditional beliefs about the incarnation, the resurrection and life after death. He is dogmatic in the sense that this is what he believes to be true but not in the sense that he is trying to ram it down my throat. He recognises that all these matters are 'essentially unknowable' and that when we talk about them the language fails but yes, Jesus was divine, the resurrection was a historical event, Jesus did rise from the dead and so shall we though in what form is a mystery beyond our understanding.

He is just across the table but we are miles apart because I do not believe in any of these things. How can I gauge whether his firm faith should encourage me to consider the possibility that God exists? I ask him whether God acts in the world and he replies that God acts through the sacraments, through baptism, for example, which creates the possibility of change for the individual, and he believes that God's influence may also be seen in historical events such as the collapse of communism, though this, he says, is a controversial view.

Father Anthony's faith and commitment to the Jesuit ideal ought to challenge my scepticism but I cannot take seriously the possibility of a God who intervenes in human affairs. So I try a different approach. I ask whether someone can be convinced by experience that God exists and I mention, not St. Paul, for who would not take God seriously in those circumstances, but my visit to the Carmelite Monastery. Sister Teresa, if I understood her correctly, became convinced of the existence of a personal God because she experienced his power to transform her life.

'Conviction must come first,' Father Anthony says, 'you cannot experience God's presence unless you are ready, as I am sure Sister Teresa was, to believe in His existence.'

That appears to be the catch. I have to believe in God before I can have the sort of experience that might persuade me to do so. Sister Teresa's faith is 'not transferable', nor is Father Anthony's.

This I anticipate will be a problem throughout my journey. I have met a few people in my life of whom I have thought, 'If he's a believer, there must be something in it' but that is not the same as understanding someone's religious faith from the inside. An example, however shining, will not be enough to persuade me so I am looking for a Christian faith that while it may not be transferable, is open enough for me to catch a glimpse of what it means to believe in God.

Father Timothy Radcliffe will not thank me for listing his credentials, partly because he is a modest man and partly because he does not believe any more than I do that a life that proclaims the existence of God has anything to do with positions held or qualifications obtained but I want to put our meeting into context. He was born into a Roman Catholic family, educated by the Benedictines at Downside and entered the Dominican Order of Preachers in 1965 at the age of twenty. He has been head of the Order's English Province, Master of the Dominican Order worldwide and Grand Chancellor of the Pontifical University of St. Thomas Aquinas in Rome. Much in demand as a preacher and almost constantly on the move around the world, I pin him down in his home base at Blackfriars in Oxford.

The Dominicans, like the Jesuits, have dark periods in their history – they are still coming to terms with their role in the Inquisition – but unlike the Jesuits, they have never had a reputation for being tricky customers. There is no Dominican equivalent of the old Spanish proverb, 'Hang a Jesuit and he'll make off with the rope'.

Father Timothy is relaxed and informal, in mufti with an open-necked shirt. In response to my explanation of why I have come, he says, 'The Christian journey is a sort of agnosticism because it is a journey towards a God we cannot grasp. That idea was at the heart of Thomas Aquinas's theology – "What God is, we cannot say." '

'Can we even say he exists?'

He takes a book from his shelves and, finding the right page, suggests that I read the first paragraph. It is from a lecture on God given by Herbert McCabe, a Dominican who had a profound influence on Father Timothy when he was an undergraduate at Oxford.

'In my view to assert that God exists is to claim the right and need to carry on an activity, to be engaged in research, and I think this throws light on what we are doing if we try to prove the existence of God. To prove the existence of God is to prove that some questions still need asking, that the world poses these question for us.'

What McCabe is saying, Father Timothy suggests, is that if we are puzzled by why anything exists at all, we may be on the road to encountering God. God could be the answer to the question, but not in the sense that Christopher Wren is the answer to why St. Paul's

Cathedral exists. The question of the existence of the universe is really about whether anything does ultimately have sense. Is there a meaning to it all? For a Christian, belief in God is like an encounter with the one who is the meaning. In faith one meets – but does not fully grasp or tie down or wrap up – the meaning of it all.

He is not trying to persuade me, only to indicate ways in which I can look at the problem. It is important, he says, not to believe in a God that no one should believe in anyway. He is talking of the God of the religious fundamentalists, an invisible powerful person, an oppressive figure. I have not met any Christian fundamentalists, literal Biblicists or extreme evangelicals, but perhaps I should do so. Father Timothy's idea of God is very different from theirs.

'God is not a very important invisible person running the universe. God is not over against us. He is present in all of us. Augustine says, "God is closer to us than we are ourselves." Or as the Muslims say, "God is closer to me than my jugular vein." He is the ground of our being, the deepest interiority of our being.'

I throw up my hands in despair while continuing to write down what he has said. I have heard this sort of language before and for the life of me, I have no idea what it means and I say so. I fear he must be regretting that he agreed to see me but he is patient and unpatronising and he shares my frustration at the inadequacy of the language. But I am not sure I would understand 'the deepest interiority of our being' even if he had the precise and accurate words to define it. If there really is a God, it should not be this difficult to explain who or what or where he is. How lustily we used to sing as schoolboys 'ineffable, invisible, God only wise' without knowing or caring what ineffable meant and now that I do know, my instinct is to say that something that cannot be expressed in words probably doesn't exist.

I try again. 'What exactly does it mean to say that God is present in us all?'

'It means that when you really know yourself, then at the heart of existing at all is the fact that you are infinitely loved. At the deepest interiority of your being, you are not a solitary individual. To be is to be given existence by the One who loves you.'

I cannot honestly say I understand.

'Is that love an emotion?' I ask.

'No'.

'What is it then?' If I sound impatient it is because I sense that if anyone can persuade me to take seriously the possibility that God exists, this man can so it is all the more frustrating if I don't understand.

'When I love, I exist more fully. I am freed from being the centre of the universe,' he explains. 'In loving God I am no longer trapped in solitude. I flourish in friendship, which Thomas Aquinas called "the most perfect form of love", because it is not possessive and seeks only the good of the other person.'

This at last is something I can understand but isn't he just talking about what Richard Dawkins would call 'unDarwinian selflessness'?

'No, it is more than that. This love is a realisation of my capacity to be.'

He has lost me again. What on earth does that mean?

He responds by having a go at Descartes. The French philosopher's famous definition of what it means to be, 'I think therefore I am', is too self-centred. What God enables us to say is, 'I am no longer the centre of the Universe, therefore I am.' It is only by loving in this sense that we are truly alive, that we realise our capacity to be.

'How do we know that this capacity for un-possessive love, for not being the centre of the Universe, is God's input to human life and not the result of blind evolution?'

'We don't but I believe it is. If you love then surely one can have a sense that this is the meaning of everything, for which we are made.'

I suppose it is possible that the evidence for God's existence lies not in the extraordinary character of the universe but in the fact that human beings have the capacity for overruling their natural self-centeredness. It all depends on where that capacity comes from and he has so nearly persuaded me to take his answer seriously, I am tempted to propose a meeting with Richard Dawkins, who lives a few hundred yards away just up the road, so that I can settle this matter once and for all but Father Timothy doubts whether such a meeting would be helpful.

'Science and theology are not in conflict,' he says, 'unless science claims a monopoly of the truth, but they are different ways of talking about the world. Science helps us understand the world in ways that are deeply fascinating and helpful. Theology uses any way, any discipline, to make sense of the universe. Not how the world works but that it exists at all is the mystery theology tries to understand. What gives meaning, what makes sense of our lives? For human beings throughout history the capacity for unpossessive love gives at least a glimpse of what our lives may be about.'

My reaction to Father Timothy's patient answers to my questions is this. I have caught a glimpse of Father Timothy's faith. I feel like a father who, seeking a lost child, sees a figure on the distant horizon and wonders whether there is a reason to hope. Before I leave I tell Father Timothy about Umberto Eco's 'room for Hope', and ask him what he hopes for and he replies. 'That in the end it will all make sense'. I say that is what I hope for too, but he knows and I know that we mean different things. Belief in the resurrection is central to his faith and his hope is that at the end the meaning of his life will be made clear to him. I have a more modest hope that at the end of my journey I shall know whether or not to believe in the possibility of God's existence.

6

IN WHICH I MEET AN ANGLICAN PRIEST WHO REJECTS TRADITIONAL CHRISTIAN DOCTRINE

It is late November and I am at the crossroads, not certain which way to turn. Father Timothy Radcliffe's case for taking seriously the possibility that God exists caught my imagination and I want to see whether it holds its attraction for me when I have met a wider variety of believers and nonbelievers.

The problem I have with Timothy's idea of God is that though he expresses it in terms of a God who is present in each one of us, he clearly believes that the word God also corresponds to an external reality, a God who is 'out there'. He told me that he was anything but a pious child and that he was nearly expelled from Downside School for reading <u>Lady Chatterly's Lover</u> during a church service but he is a cradle Catholic. God has always been there for him and he has never doubted God's existence. What I want to know is whether his God is accessible to someone who cannot believe in a God 'out there' or in the supernatural trappings of Christianity.

This particular enquiry may be a dead end but I have read in Julian Baggini's <u>A Very Short Introduction to Atheism,</u> that there is an Anglican priest who has tried to save something distinctive from the wreckage of religious belief by advocating a form of Christianity with the supernatural element taken out. The subject of Baggini's somewhat backhanded compliment is Reverend Don Cupitt, sometime Dean of Emmanuel College, Cambridge. The fact that Cupitt is regarded by some traditional Christians as a missionary who has gone native, an atheist in all but name, whets my appetite. Forty years ago they said the same about John Robinson, the Bishop of Woolwich, whose book, <u>Honest to God</u> I read with great excitement because it, too, seemed to offer the possibility of being a Christian without having to believe in all the supernatural stuff.

We meet in Cupitt's rooms in Emmanuel. He sits on an upright wooden chair that he tilts back against the bookcase so that for much of the time he appears to be suspended precariously in mid-air.

'Do you believe in timeless truths and timeless values?' He asks straightaway. I do not have a chance to think of my answer as he launches into an explanation of what he calls his 'non-realist doctrine', 'non-realist' because for him the word God does not describe a real God. There is no real God, he says, if by God you mean a person, a supernatural being who is beyond and independent of the Universe.

I have no difficulty with that though I can hear Father Timothy saying that no serious theologian has ever thought of God as a person, and I find the word 'non-realist' confusing. Just to be clear, I ask whether he believes in the existence of any God and, as I should have known, that is the wrong question. 'The right question' he tells me 'is what do you mean by God?' Exactly what he does mean is elusive and I hope I can do justice his carefully thought out answer.

I will not attempt to summarise the philosophy tutorial with which he begins. 'Belief in a real God ceased to be a live option for the ablest people after the time of Kant and Hegel', he says. I nod and look sheepish like an undergraduate who has failed to study the recommended texts, but as he continues to talk of his heroes, the philosophers who tried to come to terms with the corrosive affect of scientific scepticism on religious belief, I understand his theme. He is saying that his rejection of the old style real God supported by supernatural myths is not a diversion from the mainstream of Christianity but the point towards which Christianity has been travelling for the last two hundred years. The institutional church – of which he is still a member – is 'running on empty' because it is still psychologically attached to the idea of a real God even though most of the clergy could not give a convincing account of what that God means to them.

So what does he mean when he uses the word God? He tells me to put out of my mind any idea of God as someone to whom I can relate and instead think of the word God in an entirely new way, as a coded way of saying, 'These are the moral values I have freely chosen without any supernatural guidance; I am entirely responsible for that choice and for the direction it gives my life. So God is my spiritual ideal.'

I am baffled. I am so used to thinking of God as a super-being with whom believers can have a personal relationship, it is impossible at first for me to grasp the idea that I can use the word God to mean the moral values I have chosen. Why use the word God at all if what you are talking about is your code of ethics, your philosophy of life? Why not be a Buddhist and have done with it? Cupitt answers that the idea of God is useful as a focus of aspiration, a reference point. Lawyers and policemen know that human justice is never perfect – but the ideal of perfect justice might go on being helpful and inspiring to us.

We struggle on. Like my mathematics master at school, he cannot understand why I cannot understand. I try a few traditional questions in the hope of striking firmer ground. Does he believe in the divinity of Jesus Christ? In the back of my mind is the priest at the deathbed of Voltaire. 'Monsieur de Voltaire, vous êtes au dernier terme de votre vie, reconnaissez-vous la divinité de Jésus-Christ?' That is surely the touchstone of Christianity. Voltaire's answer was 'Laissez-moi mourir en paix,' but Cupitt is more direct. Jesus was human not divine but he embodies our values and our religious ideal so that the myth of the incarnation still has importance for us.

'Do you believe in life after death?'

'No, we are re-cycled in this world.' He has no illusions about our mortality or about the ultimate extinction of all life on earth but despite this bleak prospect he still believes our human existence can have meaning if we make a creative choice to be responsible for the moral direction of our lives. And suddenly and unexpectedly, I am on his wavelength. What he is saying, to use his religious language, is that it is an act of faith if, faced with extinction, we do not despair but respond positively by choosing to be responsible for the moral direction of our lives. God, therefore, can be said to be the sum of our moral values because it is those moral values and not a supernatural super being that will give meaning to our lives.

I still think he is talking about a philosophy of life and not about a religion but I am afraid of becoming entangled in a debate about the meaning of words and I want to ask him where our moral values come from. I remember that Cardinal Martini, in one of his letters to Umberto Eco, argues that moral values cannot be sustained unless they are founded on metaphysical principles or on a personal God. Cupitt will have none of this. He is sure our moral values have evolved by trial and error, that they are man-made and not dictated from beyond.

Don Cupitt and traditional doctrine in the form of Cardinal Martini are so far apart it is difficult to believe that Christianity can contain them both but Cupitt insists that he has not left Christianity, it is the other Christians who are not yet ready to embrace a faith free from superstition. He is the front-runner showing Christianity the way it will have to go. No wonder he finds it difficult to get his books published by religious presses in Britain – his latest books were published in California – and that even fellow Anglicans who are by no means traditionalist find his idea of God difficult to swallow. Twenty years ago, Rowan Williams, the present Archbishop of Canterbury, commenting on Cupitt's use of God language wrote, 'I believe his account of religion is profoundly irreligious.'

I am attracted to Don Cupitt's interpretation of Christian doctrine because it does not require me to believe in things I cannot believe in but it does not give me access to Timothy Radcliffe's God. Maybe I lack the subtlety of mind to understand Cupitt fully and I certainly lack his knowledge of the philosophers who have influenced him – Nietzsche, Kierkegaard and Wittgenstein are just names in the index to me – but I do not see his religion, if religion it is, as an alternative to agnosticism or to atheism for that matter. For Cupitt, Jesus is the embodiment of his religious ideal but, as I have discovered, an atheist, too, may see in the life and teaching of Jesus a striking instance of 'unDarwinian selflessness'. If I am going to abandon agnosticism, which I still do not feel inclined to do, it will have to be for atheism or for an idea of God that is more than just a code word for a commitment to a moral life.

7

IN WHICH I MEET THREE ATHEISTS

Ever since meeting Richard Dawkins I have been asking myself why, if I do not believe in the existence of God, I am not an atheist. The answer I give is that I am not ready to commit myself one way or the other but behind that answer is a prejudice that Richard Dawkins' reasonableness has not entirely dispelled. How much easier it is to say, 'I am an agnostic' if anyone asks, rather than confessing to atheism. So I am going to meet three more atheists in the hope that they will encourage me to judge atheism on its merits.

I first heard Professor Peter Atkins speak in a debate with Dr Wesley Carr, the Dean of Westminster, and what sticks in my memory is the uncompromising firmness with which he used the word 'annihilation'. Death is the end and what awaits us is annihilation; to believe anything else is wishful thinking.

Peter is Professor of Chemistry at Oxford and we meet in his rooms in Lincoln College. It turns out that he, too, was at that public meeting in Conway Hall but I decide not to ask what he thought of the cartoon mocking religion. Instead, I ask, 'What is the basis of your atheism?' but once again I have asked the wrong question. The first question to ask, he tells me, is 'What is the basis for belief?' His answer is simple. There is no evidence for the existence of God so he does not believe. His atheism is lean and minimalist. If God is not known to exist, it is not necessary to suppose that he does.

A glint in his eye makes me suspect that he enjoys provoking theologians even more than Dawkins does so I ask how his atheism affects his life as a teacher and a member of the college. He is sad, he says, to see intelligent young people on their knees and he objects to money being spent on the chapel and on theology when it could be spent on more worthwhile things. 'A decent chemist is twenty times more use than any poet,' says Bazavov, Turgenev's nihilist in his novel <u>Father and Sons</u> and although Peter Atkins does not say a decent chemist is twenty times more use than any theologian, I can imagine that is what he thinks. He does say however that he has 'scored pretty well on chaplains' and goes on to explain that he has helped to persuade some of the college chaplains to abandon the Church of England. One of the chaplains he did not persuade was Robin Griffiths-Jones, a former pupil of mine and now Master of the Temple church in London. I must ask Robin how he resisted Peter Atkins' arguments.

There is something refreshingly direct about Peter's atheism. He makes no bones about his hostility to religion which he sees not as a harmless eccentricity but as a malign force in the world. 'If there were a God', he says,' it would be the Devil.' He scorns the idea that there can be a dialogue between science and religion, they are oil and water and can never mix; if there are leading scientists who believe in God that can probably be explained by cultural conditioning or genetic disposition.

His atheism has its origins in his experience as a young scientist discovering that there is a rational explanation for things that once seemed mysterious, and this scientific optimism (he says he leaves pessimism to the philosophers) still underpins his atheism; a time will come when 'there is nothing that cannot be understood, nothing that cannot be explained.' So his atheism is not an irrational hostility to religion but an unusually confident belief that all the remaining mysteries of the universe will be solved.

'Even why anything exists at all?'

'Yes, even that.'

That I find hard to believe because why anything exists at all is a philosophical question not a scientific one but we have come so far and discovered so much, I can see no logical reason to doubt that all the scientific questions at least will one day be answered.

Unlike Peter Atkins, the next atheist I meet recognises that something of value would be lost if religion disappeared altogether. Julian Baggini, is an author and free lance journalist and editor of The Philosopher's Magazine. We meet in London at Mario's café in Lower Regent Street and because it is late on Friday afternoon the café is crowded with people relaxing with friends and looking forward to the weekend. We find two seats in the corner but the tables are so close that our conversation is easily overheard and the man at the next table looks up from his evening paper and frowns when he hears the word 'God' as though he wishes us to know that there is a time and place for everything.

I tell Julian how much I enjoyed reading his A very short Introduction to Atheism' but also how profoundly I disagreed with his criticism of agnostics for sitting on the fence. His case for atheism and against agnosticism hinges on the idea of 'defeasibility', a word I have not heard before. He explains that a belief is said to be defeasible if the possibility remains open that it is wrong. He is convinced that there is no evidence for the existence of God but he accepts that there is a possibility that he may be wrong.

I say, 'Then you are an agnostic not an atheist?'

Julian disagrees. He is making a distinction between dogmatic atheism, which believes it cannot possibly be wrong, and his undogmatic atheism which is a firmly held belief but one that recognises the remote possibility that convincing evidence for the existence of God might cause him to change his mind. He cannot be an agnostic because on the evidence available now, God does not exist so there is no reason for him to suspend judgement and sit on the fence.

The clatter and chatter of Mario's Café at the end of the working week make it difficult to think through the implications of Julian's distinction between dogmatic and undogmatic atheism. Is it a real distinction or is he just trying to give atheism a friendly face? If there is such a thing as his provisional, undogmatic atheism then the difference between that and my agnosticism is only a matter of emphasis. Neither of us thinks that there is any credible evidence for the existence of God but we both accept that as the reason why anything exists at all is unknowable it is possible that we are wrong. He calls that position undogmatic atheism, I call it agnosticism.

I order two more cappuccinos and we reflect on what would be lost if religion disappeared. 'On balance, I would rather religion was not there,' Julian says, 'but if we dismiss it all as nonsense we are missing something. These are intelligent people and their religion enables them to orientate themselves to the world in a positive way.'

He was brought up as a Christian but was put off by the orchestrated evangelical rallies he attended as a teenager. The idea of God as a judge seemed to him ridiculous. There was no moment when he knew he had become an atheist; as belief faded and died, he no longer thought it was important whether God existed or not. He is wary of zealots, by which he means of both militant atheists and religious fundamentalists, and on this at least we are in agreement.

Lewis Wolpert calls himself a dogmatic atheist but a less fanatical man would be hard to find. He was until recently Professor of Biology as applied to medicine at University College, London, the 'Godless College' established to break the Church of England's monopoly of higher education. We meet over lunch in the senior common room where talk of atheism is unlikely to cause any surprise.

Lewis was brought up in a Jewish family in South Africa, learnt Hebrew at school and had his bar mitzvah at the age of thirteen. As with other atheists I have met, he experienced no sudden loss of religion just a growing certainty that there was no evidence for the existence of God. He says that he is a dogmatic atheist in the sense that he has no doubts about the non-existence of God but he will not demean or attack religion unless a religion tries to impose its views on him, and he has no wish to change what other people think. One of his sons is a born again Christian. As a leading scientist he is aware of how much we do not understand especially about the origins of life but this does not persuade him to question his atheism. His attitude towards those scientists who see evidence of a divine presence in the universe is typical of his open-minded and clear-headed approach. He speaks well of their scientific achievements, he respects their religious beliefs and he dismisses as pointless their attempts to reconcile science and religion.

If I ever decide to be an atheist, I hope I shall be as tolerant an atheist as he is. He is amused by the English attitude to atheism 'They are not so much prejudiced against it as embarrassed by it,' he says, and we conjure up a Batemen cartoon of horrified faces at the dinner table, 'The man who confessed to being an atheist.' But will I really refuse to become an atheist just because it is socially embarrassing? There must be more to it than that but having met these three atheists I am hard pushed to say what it is that holds me back.

David :

Atheists have no sense of depth
to the meaning of life.
Scientists in particular shouldn't
have a closed mind.

8

IN WHICH I MEET THREE ANGLICAN PRIESTS WHO HAVE NOT REJECTED TRADITIONAL BELIEFS

If I decide to become a Roman Catholic I am pretty certain I shall be told what it is that the Catholic Church believes. Although Sister Teresa, Father Anthony and Father Timothy, gave different accounts of their relationship with God, they were all speaking from within the framework of Catholic doctrine. I was particularly struck by the phrase Sister Teresa used when I asked her about life after death and she replied, 'My natural reaction is that death is the end but I choose to believe the Church's teaching.' But if I decide to return to the Church of England in which I was confirmed over forty years ago, will I be told what the church's teaching is or are the rumours true that the Church of England no longer knows what it believes?

I am early for my appointment with David Stancliffe, the Anglican Bishop of Salisbury, so I spend half and hour in the magnificent gothic cathedral, evidence that Thomas Aquinas's contemporaries in thirteenth century England had no need of proof of the existence of God. Two elderly gentlemen with silver hair and wearing blue gowns offer to show me round but I set off on my own and find the modern east window which is dedicated to Amnesty International and Prisoners of Conscience. How many Christians in the country would go to prison, I wonder, if under a totalitarian regime, believing in the existence of God was a criminal offence? The cynic in me says very few but I am not sure about that and it would be very interesting to know at what question the Christians would dig in their heals. Reconnaisez-vous la divinite de Jesus-Christ?

David Stancliffe and I have known one another a long time but we meet seldom. For eleven years, he has been Bishop of Salisbury, a vast diocese that stretches as far west as Weymouth and includes the South Dorset Jurassic Coast whose fossils helped to discredit once and for all the Church's time-table for creation.

We talk in David's study where I note that Anglican priests are more inclined than Roman Catholic to line their walls with books. This may be just because they are better paid but David's floor to ceiling bookshelves, filled like an old apothecary's shop with every possible remedy, suggests that Anglican priests are more in need of reassurance because there is no distinctive Anglican doctrine. When I ask David whether there will be a life after death and he replies simply and honestly, 'I don't know', he does not add, as Sister Teresa did, 'but I choose to believe the Church's teaching'.

Don Cupitt told me that he thought the Church of England was 'running on empty' because the spurious consolations of traditional belief had been irretrievably lost so I am interested to know how much traditional belief David is prepared to stand by.

'Do you believe in the divinity of Jesus Christ?'

'Jesus was a hundred per cent human and a hundred per cent divine,' he replies.

I do not think that answer would keep him out of prison or satisfy the priest at the deathbed of Voltaire.

'What does that mean exactly?'

'It is our human vocation to be divine', he says, 'to see in Jesus what we are capable of being. Jesus is divine in the sense that he is what God wishes us to be, yet he must also be wholly human if we are to have any hope of following his example.'

This is a characteristic Anglican response – intelligent, sophisticated and sufficiently ambiguous to hide the fact that the Church of England is no longer certain that Jesus was anything other than a human being.

'What happened at the resurrection?' I ask.

'If nothing happened, as the demythologisers claim, then it is difficult to account for the extraordinary development of Christianity.'

Once again, the image of the retreating army come to mind. The high command, that is to say the bishops of the Church of England, know perfectly well that it is no longer possible to believe that Jesus was divine and that he defied the laws of nature by rising from the dead but they are afraid of spreading panic in the ranks. Who can blame them? They have a job to do and that is to maintain order and morale in the pews as the Church withdraws from its traditional beliefs. So I am not surprised when David changes the direction of our conversation and tells me that what is important to him in his Christian life is not whether he believes propositions about the resurrection or the divinity of Jesus but the quality of his relationship with God and with other people.

'Jesus did not offer us a systematic theology to believe in,' he says, 'but an invitation to follow him. Only by risking engaging with him and with other people can we avoid being trapped inside ourselves and discover the possibility of a love in which we seek nothing for ourselves.'

That I can understand but I wonder whether David's Christianity amounts to anything more than what Don Cupitt calls 'disinterested morality with religious myth as an aid to this.' I probably do him and his church an injustice by suggesting that Anglicanism is in full retreat, but David is too honest to deny that on some key questions of Christian doctrine he is just not sure.

Robin Griffiths-Jones enjoys the grant title of the Reverend and Valiant Master of the Temple. His medieval church was built by the Crusaders, who were not noted for their disinterested morality, on ground between Fleet Street and the Thames and now serves the lawyers of the two Inns of Court, the Inner and Middle Temple. Before moving to the Temple, Robin was the chaplain of Lincoln College, Oxford so I ask him how he got on with Professor Peter Atkins, the college's resident atheist. 'We agreed to differ,' he replies. Far from finding that his work as Chaplain was undermined, Robin thought that Atkins was his best recruiting sergeant because the Professor's very public atheism seemed to have the effect of encouraging more undergraduates to attend chapel services.

We meet in Oxford where Robin is using sabbatical leave to write a study of the Resurrection. He has previously written a book on the four gospel writers, of whom Luke is his favourite. 'For Luke, more than for the other gospel writers' he tells me, 'Jesus is the ideal, the infinitely attractive example.'

'He is an infinitely attractive example but that does not prove that God exists.'

'We are all made in the image of God,' Robin says. 'Jesus is the unsullied image. We are the sullied image.'

I like the idea of Jesus as the unsullied image of God if by God we mean the ideal and nothing more. Heavens, I am beginning to sound like Don Cupitt. I ask Robin why we need the idea of God at all.

'Because it is dangerous to think that you can just admire Jesus' ethic. Without God, you make man the measure of all things and that leads to our arrogance and complacency. We need a focus outside ourselves to understand the true nature of Jesus' teaching. If you let God go, you let love go. God is love.'

'What does that mean exactly?'

'It means that love is the creative power underlying the universe as well as the deepest truth about our humanity.'

Does he mean that the capacity to love without asking anything in return is what proves that we are made in the image of God and that this is the key to understanding our place in the universe? With Robin, as with other Christians I have talked to, I have the tantalising sense of almost understanding but not quite. Out of the corner of my eye, I catch a glimpse of his meaning but when I turn, it has gone. How frustrating this pursuit of God is. It is not just that the devil has the best tunes; the atheists seem to have by far the clearest explanations. They can reduce their case to clear and unequivocal language whereas Christians like Robin and Timothy Radcliffe are more like poets, struggling at the borders of what can be said. Robin argues that attempts to deny the existence of God are just as incoherent but the ball is not in the atheists' court. They do not need to prove the non-existence of God; all they have to do is to argue that the evidence for the existence of God lacks credibility. If God exists, show me.

Robin recognises my difficulty and I recognise his. When we talk about God, we do not know what we are talking about so that when I ask him whether he is using the words God and love to mean the same thing and he replies that God is just a useful name for the love that he believes is the deepest truth about the universe and about ourselves, we both understand that we are playing blind man's buff. The very logic of our language cannot capture God.

It is a relief to hear him talk about his work. 'Jesus was utterly alien to the world he came into,' he says, 'and the gospel writers are trying to open our eyes to the extraordinary claims that Jesus made. The trouble is we have domesticated the gospels and we don't recognise how original Jesus was.' I recall that Richard Dawkins thought that only by separating Jesus from the supernatural nonsense could we recognise his originality and I wonder how much of the 'supernatural nonsense' Robin believes.

Like Sister Teresa, he is in two minds about death. When his parents died, he had no sense of their continuing presence and he thinks that by right, we should expect death to be the end. It is God's will that we should grow old and die. But he finds it hard to believe that God who is love will allow us to be utterly extinguished.

I ask whether he recognises the divinity of Jesus Christ and he replies: 'Jesus is the total and perfect self-disclosure of God in human terms. We call the creative power God the Father and his self-disclosure God the Son.' He smiles apologetically: 'It sounds like an ancient and alien code, I know but we have never found a better way of saying it.' I want to put my conversations with David and Robin into some sort of perspective. Have I really understood anything that they said? This much I think I have understood. They both believe, as Timothy Radcliffe does, that our capacity for unpossessive love is the key to our humanity and that we cannot tap into that capacity without God's help. But I am not convinced that we all do have this capacity for unpossessive love and I do not understand how, if we do, it throws any light on the possible existence of God.

It is probably just as well, that soon after talking with two Anglican priests who emphasise that God is love, I am given a stern warning by another Anglican priest that God is also our judge and that we shall all stand before him one day to give an account of our lives.

The Reverend Prebendary Sandy Millar is the vicar of Holy Trinity Brompton in London's Knightsbridge and the founder of the phenomenally successful Alpha Courses that have breathed new life in Christian churches across the world. The evangelical style of these courses is not to everyone's taste but there is no doubting their effectiveness.

We meet over a simple lunch in the vicarage behind the church. Sandy is in his sixties; silver-haired and soft-spoken, he looks like a favourite uncle rather than the man who has launched one of the most dynamic and influential Christian initiatives of modern times. The Alpha Courses, which Sandy started at Holy Trinity Brompton in the 1970s, were designed to teach the parishioners the basics of the Christian faith and then were developed in the 1990s by another Holy Trinity clergyman, Nicky Gumbel, as a tool for worldwide evangelism. This is Christianity that is most definitely not on the defensive. It sets out, confident in its beliefs, to strengthen existing members of the church and to win new recruits for Christ. Alpha Courses are currently running in one hundred and fifty countries and six million people have completed an Alpha Course. Sandy Millar's local initiative has become Alpha International, a highly effective organisation, skilled in marketing and communications.

Sandy tells me that thirty years ago he identified a hunger among young adults who wanted to know what being a Christian involved so that they could make up their own minds whether or not they were interested. But how could they find out? They couldn't very well ask questions during a church service and they were reluctant to go to the vicar on an individual basis. The Alpha Courses gave them the opportunity to join other people, who wanted to ask the same questions, to belong before they had to believe. The course now lasts ten weeks and those who join can complete the whole course without having to make any commitment. 'What young people want to know,' Sandy says, 'is not is it true but does it work.' The course gives them the chance to discover in open discussion and without embarrassment whether belief in God is likely to work for them.

I am interested because all along I have thought that it was impossible to sample Christianity without believing the unbelievable but Sandy seems to be saying that it is possible to find out whether it works without believing that it is true. Or is he saying that the more you are convinced that it is true, the more likely you are to find that it works? As we talk on, I realise that it is the latter and that I would have to sign up to certain beliefs before I enjoyed the benefits.

What Sandy means by 'true' is what is revealed in the bible. He knows that the bible is the word of God and he distinguishes between those Christians who, when they need help or guidance, reach for the bible and those who don't. He reaches for the bible.

Do you recognise the divinity of Jesus Christ? For Sandy and for those who have completed an Alpha Course, that is not a question that presents any difficulty. They believe that Jesus was the Son of God because the gospels leave them no doubt. The miracles he performed are recorded, the evidence for his resurrection is overwhelming, and there is no doubt that those who believe in him will have eternal life, it says so in St John's Gospel, chapter eleven, verses 25 and 26. 'I am the resurrection and the life: he that believeth in me, though he were dead, yet shall he live. And whosoever liveth and believeth in me shall never die.'

'And for those who do not believe?'

'The greatest sin is unbelief,' Sandy replies. 'It is a mistake to think that you can treat Jesus as just an inspiring religious teacher. Most people who say they agree with the ethics of the Sermon on the Mount have never read that part of the gospels where Jesus warns us that we all face God's judgment and that those who have failed to respond to him in this life will face eternal punishment in the next.'

I have been here before, long ago, as a young boy aged ten attending the Crusaders, an evangelical Sunday school in South London. There was the same literal reading of the bible, the same promise of eternal life for those who come forward to commit themselves to Jesus and the same unstated threat of damnation for those who didn't. My older brother and I sat tight as others went forward to join the ranks of the Elect.

When it is time for me to leave, Sandy asks, 'Would you be offended if I pray for you?'

He means here and now, so we stand together as he asks God to guide me. I am neither offended nor embarrassed. I think of myself as a visitor from another world who should respect the local customs.

For several months now I have been seeking evidence for the existence of God and I decided some time ago that one convincing piece of evidence might be the example of men and women whose lives had been transformed by their faith. From what Sandy Millar tells me, the Alpha Courses have transformed for the better thousands of lives, particularly of young adults, the average age of those attending the courses being twenty-seven, so why as I say goodbye to him and walk away into the December dusk passed the bright shop windows of Knightsbridge filled with expensive Christmas gifts, do I remain sceptical?

One answer is that I have a deep-rooted suspicion of evangelism that dates from my boyhood experience of the Crusaders. But I have a more rational objection to the Alpha approach. I cannot take seriously the argument that it must be true because it says so in the bible. That sort of literal biblicism will never be for me. But I can see its attractions. For Alpha graduates, as those who have completed the course are called, there is no protracted intellectual debate about the meaning of the word God or about whether the resurrection is a metaphor. In the words of Nicky Gumbel, who has taken over from Sandy Millar as the driving force in Alpha International, Alpha graduates 'have found

God as their Father, Jesus Christ as their Saviour and Lord and the Holy Spirit as the one who comes to live within them.'

I have no reason to question the genuineness of the Alpha graduates' conversion or to doubt them when they say, as they do, 'I am the happiest I've ever been in my life now that I want to do things that God wants me to do,' but I think that the transformation of their lives is evidence of the effectiveness of Alpha's evangelism not of the existence of God. The Alpha courses will continue to change people's lives whether God exists or not but I will accept Sandy Millar's invitation to attend the first day of an Alpha course in January if only to prove to myself that I am not afraid of being converted.

9

We are spending Christmas in a small family hotel behind the Pantheon in the heart of old Rome where there are narrow cobbled streets and layers of history. Next to the hotel, in the Piazza Minerva, is the Dominican Church of Santa Maria Sopra Minerva, built on the site of a Roman temple, and in the centre of the piazza, an obelisk that once stood in front of a temple to the Egyptian god, Isis.

This holiday is a time for me to reflect on the past five months. Since I started my journey in July, I have swung this way and that, one day drawn to Timothy Radcliffe's idea that the peculiarly human capacity for unpossessive love is evidence of God's presence and the next wondering why I am not an atheist. A few days before leaving for Rome I came across a quotation that accurately reflected the fluctuating nature of my journey so far. It is from a book called The Evolution of Darwin's Religious Views and it reads:

'His beliefs concerning the possible existence of some sort of God never entirely ceased to ebb and flow, nor did his evaluation of the merits of such beliefs. At low tide, so to speak, he was essentially an undogmatic atheist; at high tide he was a tentative theist; the rest of the time he was basically agnostic – in sympathy with theism but unable or unwilling to commit himself on such imponderable questions.'

On the afternoon of Christmas Eve we climb the Capitoline Hill to see the bronze equestrian statue of Marcus Aurelius, emperor and philosopher. I have a particular reason for wanting to see this famous statue. Before I started on my journey, I wrote to a Jesuit friend in Edinburgh, Father Jack Mahoney, asking his advice on who I should see and what I should read and to my surprise he recommended that before I set off I should read the <u>Meditations</u> of Marcus Aurelius. So I did and found myself entirely in sympathy with emperor's brand of stoicism and especially with his attitude to death. Over and over again he urges the calm acceptance of death as 'a process of nature which only children can be afraid of.' Undistracted by false hopes of survival, he sees dying as one of our assignments in life. 'You boarded, set sail, you made your passage, time to disembark.' This is the ideal I aspire to but whether I shall be able to achieve it when the harbour comes into view, I do not know. And here he is, a true philosopher-king, riding high over the city of Rome nearly two thousand years after his death. What I cannot understand is why a Jesuit should recommend an author who has tended to confirm my agnosticism.

My wife Daphne is a Roman Catholic and because it is Christmas Eve, I go with her to Midnight Mass at Santa Maria Sopra Minerva. The church is so vast, the congregation of a hundred or so appears small. Once again I am a visitor from another world, letting my mind wander round a church that is rich in history and where Timothy Radcliffe must have officiated at many services when he was Master of the Dominican Order. The Renaissance pope, Leo X, is buried here and the deeply religious painter, Fra Anglico, who was so overcome by emotion when painting Christ on the Cross tears poured down his face. In a marble sarcophagus under the high altar is the body of St. Catherine of Siena or rather, most of her body, her head being in Siena because the Sienese claimed her as their own. The bones of saints mean nothing to me but, although I once occupied Oliver Cromwell's rooms in Cambridge, I have no urge to cast these holy relics into the nearest ditch, on the contrary I feel protective of them. I am far less offended by harmless superstition than by cheap laughs at superstition's expense.

As the mass proceeds at its leisurely pace, I think about St. Catherine of Siena. When Timothy Radcliffe was asked whether there were figures in Dominican history to whom he was drawn, he replied, 'I find Catherine of Siena immensely attractive.' I know little about her other than that, almost single-handed, she ended the Babylonish captivity of the papacy in Avignon by persuading Pope Gregory 1X to return to Rome. What is it with these Roman Catholic women who achieve sainthood by combining mysticism with shrewdness and great practical ability? Was that their way of transcending but not disrupting the control of the male-dominated church? I tell myself that I would have liked to test my agnosticism against their faith but I am not sure whether, if St Catherine appeared now in the pew beside me which is empty as the others have gone up to receive the body of Christ, I should have the confidence to take her on.

On Christmas Day we walk to the Vatican and stand in front of the great façade of St. Peter's in the pouring rain, waiting with hundreds of other to hear the Pope's blessing in many languages. In front of us a group of nuns hold brightly coloured umbrellas and beside them children bare-headed on their father's shoulders seem oblivious of the weather. At the back of the vast crowd a large banner is being held up above the umbrellas with the message 'L'Immacolata Vincera.' Every few minutes, the well-practised shouts of young people calling for the Holy Father give the occasion the flavour of a political rally and when at last Pope John Paul 11 appears, hunched in his popemobile, the applause is accompanied by shrieks of delight. He is their hero and their hope and for millions throughout the world he is their reassurance that seeking God is not a wild goose chase. As he ploughs through the blessings, one language after another, his voice heavy with the effort, Daphne decides to stay put but I retreat to the shelter of Bernini's colonnade where two young priests in well-cut black overcoats are reading their breviaries out of the rain.

How do I account for the resilience of Christianity? At the last count there were nearly two billion self-proclaimed Christians, that is about one third of humanity. In the United States, the world's most scientifically advanced society, ninety percent of the population pray for God's intervention and believe that God cares for them. The only explanation that makes sense to me is that religion survives and flourishes because it works; and by that I do not mean that religious propositions about a supernatural God are true but that belief in them secures benefits for believers that cannot be secured in any other way. I am thinking of the two aspects of the human condition that religion addresses. One is the need to neutralise the impact of our unbridled self-interest and the other is the need to ease our anxiety about death. Religion meets both these needs by proposing a higher authority that underwrites a disinterested morality and promises that death is not the end. Death is religion's trump card. Given the choice between Marcus Aurelius's calm acceptance that death is the end and religion's offer of hope that it is not, the hundreds standing here in the rain, waiting for the chance to cheer the pope's use of their own language, will abandon common sense and choose hope. But not me. I may decide to believe in God for all sorts of reasons but not because I am afraid of dying.

Boxing Day in Rome is the Feast of St, Stephen who was stoned to death because he said he saw Jesus standing at God's right hand. In the evening we hear the first reports of a disaster in the Indian Ocean following an earthquake under the sea but it is only over the next few days that the scale of the death and destruction becomes clear. Some people will greet this natural disaster with the cry, 'Why does God allow such things to happen?' If I believed in God, I hope I would have the sense to realise that having set the universe in motion God cannot prevent the natural laws operating and that a major disaster casts no more doubt on the existence of a 'First Cause God' than a man struck by lightening or a child dying of leukaemia.

But if a natural disaster is no evidence one way or the other for the existence of God, why have I been haunted since I met Martin Rees at the start of my journey by the thought that one day, however distant, the sun will die and the earth too and the universe will continue on its way as if the human race with all its follies and achievements had never been? That will be the ultimate natural disaster and how anyone can reconcile that with belief in a God who takes an interest in our destiny I cannot imagine. When on All Saints Day in 1755, an earthquake destroyed the city of Lisbon and killed thousands of people many of whom were in church at the time, Voltaire called it 'a terrible argument against optimism'. What is going to happen in six billion years may seem too remote to bother with but it is a terrible argument against optimism all the same.

On our last day in Rome we have come to the Church of Santa Maria della Vittoria which was built to celebrate the Roman Catholic victory over the Protestants at the Battle of the White Mountain in 1620. I have never thought that the way Protestants and Roman Catholics slaughtered one another was an argument against the existence of God and I am not here to re-enforce my agnosticism. I am drawn to Santa Maria della Vittoria by Bernini's famous sculpture of the Ecstasy of Saint Teresa.

I shall be leaving Rome a floating voter still where the existence of God is concerned but, as the police say when they are baffled, I have a number of lines of inquiry that I am pursuing and one of these is whether the sort of religious experiences that St. Teresa claimed to have had are evidence that I should consider.

The real St. Teresa, like St. Catherine of Siena, was a woman of such intelligence and down-to-earth good sense that it is almost impossible to imagine that she experienced visions and ecstasies. Bernini has got round this problem by portraying her, not as the tough-minded reformer of the Carmelite monasteries, but as a beautiful young woman ecstatic at the prospect of her heart being pierced by a spear thrown by an angel.

I do not want a psychiatrist to tell me what is going on here. I want to understand the nature of all St. Teresa's religious experiences especially her divine locutions when she heard God speaking to her and those occasions when she became aware of Christ's presence beside her. It is the contrast between these religious experiences and the character of the woman herself that intrigues me. Are her experiences the creation of an intensely religious imagination or evidence of a different reality beyond the material world of space and time? Heaven knows how I shall be able to answer that question unless St. Teresa appears to me in a vision as she did apparently to numerous Carmelite nuns after her death. In the meantime I have a date with the first evening of the Alpha course back in London.

10

IN WHICH I ATTEND THE FIRST SESSION OF AN ALPHA COURSE

I t is a long way from Rome to Holy Trinity Brompton but the first evening of the Alpha course raises the same question in my mind about the remarkable resilience of religion. The Church of England may be in the doldrums but when I arrive at Holy Trinity Brompton the church is crowded with three hundred young people whose average age I would say is between twenty-five and thirty.

The large Victorian church has recently been redecorated and modernised. There are no pews and this evening the nave, aisle and gallery are filled with tables for supper. It is a cheerfully welcoming scene. Young people are milling about collecting their food and finding their group table, while I go up to the gallery to join the Visitor's Group which is almost entirely made up of German Reformed Church ministers and their wives. When I explain that I am an agnostic who has come to see what the Alpha Course is all about the minister from the Ruhr sitting next to me smiles and looks puzzled.

Each group has a leader who has completed the course. Tom, our leader, works in the City and as I look down from my position in the gallery I have the impression that the audience (or is it a congregation?) is white, middle class and 'working in London', with a narrow majority of young women. As well as group leaders there are numerous helpers and one of these is Pauline who took the course fourteen years ago and has never looked back. She tells me that she was lonely and adrift in London when she met an older woman who advised her, 'My dear, you must do Alpha.' Pauline thought she would give it a try because there was a chance she 'might meet some rich Knightsbridge bloke'. She didn't but she did find Jesus and that, she says, changed her life.

We help ourselves to supper, for which a contribution of £3.50 is suggested, and then settle down to listen to Nicky Gumbel, Sandy Millar's right hand man, who will introduce the course and to-night's theme which is 'Who is Jesus?' For those who do not have a direct or close view of the low stage where Gumbel is standing at the microphone, there are television screens at key points as well as a large screen behind the speaker.

Nicky Gumbel is in his fifties, a slim, athletic figure who, Pauline whispers, is an excellent squash player. He is wearing jeans, an open necked shirt and a dark blue sweater. He talks quietly with the occasional joke but none of the rhetorical tricks, forced bonhomie and ready smiles that I associate with the word evangelism. If this is evangelism, it is of the understated English kind. He goes out of his way to emphasise that there is no pressure and that most of the people here to-night just want to know what Christianity is all about.

Before his talk, he introduces two young guitarists who step forward and greet the audience in unison, 'Hi guys', and we all stand to sing two hymns, one an old stalwart – 'Ponder anew, what the Almighty can do' – and the other a modern hymn that few of us know though the words come up on the screen and we do our best to match them with the tune.

'Who is Jesus?' Gumbel is a natural and I cannot help admiring his style that holds the attention of the young people for just under an hour. He speaks first about his own experience. His father was a German Jew and an agnostic, his mother nominally Church of England. At Oxford, where he read law, he was a non-believer and knew little about what Christians believed and this youthful agnosticism enables him to identify with his audience. He understands their doubts because he has been there too.

With his bible open in his left hand he gives us 'the intellectual basis for Christianity,' backing up each proposition with the evidence just like a barrister addressing a jury. We will find, he tells us, that the evidence supports 'the Christian contention that Jesus was and is the unique Son of God,' and we do not have to take his word for it because the evidence is there in front of us in the bible. Members of the jury have been lent bibles for the evening so that they can check the evidence for themselves. We know Jesus was the Son of God because he said he was and his claim is confirmed by his miracles, by the fact that his life and death fulfilled three hundred prophesies, above all by the fact that he rose from the dead.

For Gumbel, as for Christians everywhere, the resurrection is the clinching argument for the divinity of Christ and he takes us carefully through the evidence from the empty tomb to the appearances to the disciples. That the appearances could not possibly have been hallucinations is shown by the fact that the risen Jesus could be touched, that he ate a piece of boiled fish and on one occasion cooked breakfast for the disciples. My scepticism may make his case for Jesus being the Son of God sound more light-weight than it was. He spoke with obvious sincerity but he was once a barrister and I think he makes a mistake in presenting the evidence as though it was the sort of evidence that would stand up in court. Belief in the resurrection is surely an act of faith and cannot be based on a weighing-up of the so-called 'evidence'.

I made a New Year resolution to accept without complaining, the destination I reach at the end of my journey but this evening at Holy Trinity Brompton has confirmed my view that if I do find my way to some sort of belief in God's existence it is unlikely to be by the Alpha route. But I am the odd man out. The young people, their heads bowed over their bibles to read the evidence, look thoughtful and attentive and I have no doubt that many of them will stay the course and, like Pauline, will still be convinced by Nicky Gumbel's case for Jesus many years hence. Unlike some sceptics I am not sorry to see intelligent young people wanting to know more about the Christian faith. Towards the end of his talk,

Gumbel tells them that their presence here to-night reflects 'the spiritual hunger at the heart of every human being' and I would very much like to ask them whether they recognise this hunger in themselves and what form it takes because I do not feel it and never have, but when we break for coffee they remain in their groups and it is clear that questions from a stranger would not be welcome. So I study the literature. Next week the theme is 'Why did Jesus die?' and the week after 'How can I be sure of my faith?' Perhaps I should hear the next two talks but I think not. I slip away into the night. Although I should not judge a ten-week course on the strength of attending the first session, I know that I will never be able to take seriously this literal interpretation of the bible. The gospels are not an eyewitness account, they are a theological statement, an attempt by the gospel writers to convince their contemporaries of the 'extra-ordinariness' of Jesus.

From time to time I meet a local Roman Catholic priest who, asking about my journey, never fails to remind me that intellectual argument will not lead me to God, and he quotes Pascal, 'It is the heart that perceives God and not the reason.' And I reply that for me and I suspect for most people, the heart (whatever that means) cannot come into play unless the reason is satisfied that there is an intellectually coherent argument for even thinking about the possibility of God's existence. Of course, the final decision to believe that human life has some purpose and some meaning beyond itself will have to be a leap of faith but short of a supernatural experience on the road to Damascus, most of us will not be prepared to make a leap of faith without a firm basis of reasonable argument to take off from. At Holy Trinity Brompton, Nicky Gumbel speaks so eloquently that it would be easy to be persuaded that he is putting forward a reasonable argument for believing in God. But he is not. If I want a reasonable argument, I shall have to look elsewhere.

David:

I naturally react "negatively" to Nicky Gumbel (like Billy Graham counterproductive)

11

IN WHICH I MEET AN EVOLUTIONARY PALAEOBIOLOGIST WHO DOES NOT RULE OUT THE IDEA OF CREATION

When I dropped Thomas Aquinas's name into the conversation once too often, Timothy Radcliffe pointed out that what I called Aquinas's proofs for the existence of God were not intended as proofs but as demonstrations of the meaning of the word God, which is why each demonstration ends with the phrase 'et hoc dicimus Deum', and this we call God. He does not set out to prove that God exists, but to show us how our use of the word God is always in the context of our attempts to understand our world.

Timothy's use of the word God in the context of his attempt to understand the world made sense to me. Nicky Gumbel's at Alpha did not. John Polkinghorne's attempts to identify God's fingerprints on the universe did not make sense to me either because I was sure that science and religion are 'clean different things' and have nothing to say to one another. I have not changed my mind on that but I am intrigued by what I have been told about a leading biologist who does not dismiss out of hand the possibility that there is an intelligent direction behind evolution. So I am back in Cambridge to see Simon Conway Morris, the Professor of Evolutionary Palaeobiology, whose baroque title means that he is exploring the evolution of life using the best primary evidence available – the fossil record.

We meet in the Department of Earth Sciences where the floor of his office is so scattered with papers it requires a balancing act to avoid treading on photocopies of articles to read and notes for lectures to be given. Simon is in his early fifties, married with two grown-up sons and he is a convinced Christian who describes himself as a high Anglican. We talk about his Christian faith and my agnosticism and it is soon clear that as well as being willing to explain his scientific insights he is keen to warn me of the dangers of remaining uncommitted. I hear the warning but I am anxious to know how he reconciles his understanding of the evolution of life with his belief in the existence of God.

His answer is that the more he understands about the incredible complexity of our 'eerily well-constructed universe', particularly in his own field of evolutionary biology, the more he is inclined to think that creation is a better explanation for the way life has evolved than the idea that we are the result of an arbitrary linking up of atoms.

As I associate the word 'creation' with fundamentalist Christians in the United States who wish to ban the teaching of evolutionary biology in schools I am puzzled but Simon is no creationist in that sense. By 'creation', he means the possibility that the extraordinary rich and fertile process of evolution may not be blind but in some sense directed and purposeful, and that if this is the case, then it would not be irrational to believe that there is an intelligence behind the process. He suggests that we consider the development of our ability to understand ourselves and the world we live in. It is possible that the emergence of human intelligence was an evolutionary accident in which case the idea of a direction behind evolution makes no sense. But if there are reasons to believe that the emergence of human intelligence was an evolutionary inevitability, then it makes sense to consider the possibility that evolution was directed towards this end, in other words, that there was an intelligence behind the process.

When I ask whether the reasons are something that a layman could understand, Simon replies that the claim that we are an accident, a mere by-product of evolution does not stand up to serious analysis and one reason for saying this that I should be able to understand is the phenomena of evolutionary convergence.

'I have no idea what that means.'

'Well, if we can demonstrate, and I think we can, that everything you need for complex intelligence has emerged more than once, if more than once life has navigated successfully against all the odds to the same solution, then the emergence of human intelligence is not an accident, it must in some way that we don't yet understand be based on a deeper structure.'

'A structure? Is that a programme or what?'

'We don't know but I think there may be a reason to believe that there is a cartography of life, a road map as well as a navigation kit and that if there is, then evolution is not blind but has a direction and a purpose.'

'Would a direction and a purpose prove the existence of God?'

'No. It would give you a choice. You can believe that life is an accident and therefore without purpose or you can consider the possibility that a roadmap or structure underpinning evolution would mean that it is not mere wishful thinking to believe that life has been given a direction and by implication one could argue a purpose.'

But by whom? I cannot remember the words of Aquinas on this point but I check them when I get home.

'Now whatever lacks knowledge cannot move towards an end unless it be directed by some being endowed with knowledge and intelligence, as the arrow is directed by the archer. Therefore some intelligent being exists by whom all natural things are directed to their end, and this we call God.'

What Simon appears to be offering is, in advertising terms, 'New improved Aquinas with scientific ingredient.' If there is a structure underpinning evolution, then Aquinas's 'intelligent being' cannot be ruled out. Et hoc dicimus Deum. And this we call God.

I follow Simon's logic but as a layman I cannot evaluate the scientific argument. What examples are there of complex intelligence emerging more than once?

'Parrots, crows, dolphins and Neanderthal man who died out without any help from Homo sapiens. There are species that are not that far behind us in evolutionary terms.'

On one level, Simon's intriguing argument is a good reason to remain an agnostic, but when I say so, he abandons science and tells me: 'You face a real risk of being damned. How unfashionable and medieval that sounds. May I add a gloss to that bald statement? First, recall Pascal's wager, the idea it is better to bet on there being a God, just in case. His argument is usually regarded as a cynical ploy, to be greeted with the usual knowing smirks. Actually the argument is much deeper. Pascal was not stupid. Second, suppose that Heaven and Hell are realities? Then you may not have infinite time to make a decision. If true, these things matter absolutely. Of course the opposition say we're trying to give children sleepless nights, but I am afraid it is not a question of bogey-men or scare tactics but responding to a coherent intellectual argument. Maintain your agnosticism if you so wish, but it is your choice, your decision, not society's, not your genes.'

'I haven't decided yet. I might stay an agnostic or plunge one way or the other.'

'You can only plunge one way. You'll never find a home in atheism.'

Simon has taken me into the heart of the debate about the relationship between science and religion. As I understand it, the debate raises two questions. The first is whether there can be any worthwhile dialogue between science and religion; and the second is whether science is in a position to endorse or deny the claims that religion makes.

On the first question, I have heard nothing on my travels that makes me doubt the wisdom of Martin Rees's definition of the relationship as peaceful co-existence but not constructive dialogue. It is religion that wants the dialogue not science. There are scientists such as John Polkinghorne, who believe dialogue can be fruitful for both parties, a view supported by the Templeton Foundation in the USA which funds research on the boundary of science and religion but the attitude of most scientists is the same as that of Martin Rees. As an outsider, I am struck by the similarity between religion's desire to be at the top table with science and the delusions of a once great power that has lost an empire and is looking for a role. The presumption of theologians that they are still a major power in the world is laughable and I have some sympathy with atheists who argue that money spent on theology departments in our universities would be better spent on 'real' subjects.

Needless to say, Simon does not agree but nor does he see much point in dialogue with materialists for whose 'strutting certainties' he has no time.

'I don't believe religion, beyond our worldly prelates, has any desire to be at a top table. The table was long ago hi-jacked by Thomas Huxley and his merry descendants. How can you have a conversation with people who lack philosophical training, are breezily ignorant of theology and by sleight of hand import design arguments into an area they declare devoid of meaning?'

But it is the second question that is important to me. I came away from my meeting with John Polkinghorne convinced that nothing science discovers about the universe can be used as evidence for or against the existence of God. Simon Conway Morris is not claiming that a structure underpinning evolution would be evidence for the existence of God. He is saying that it would provide 'an intellectually coherent argument' for keeping an open mind. We have a choice. Either life is an accident and without purpose or it has been given a direction and by implication a purpose.

I have two problems with this. First, I have no idea whether Simon's case for a road-map or structure underpinning evolution will ever be taken seriously by his fellow scientists. Secondly, although Simon says that a structure underpinning evolution would not prove the existence of God, he is using the possibility of a structure to introduce into the material world of science, the religious concept of a God who gives a direction and purpose to life; and I believe that the two can't mix, that science and religion are oil and water, and that Simon's case for keeping an open mind must therefore be flawed.

12

IN WHICH I ATTEND A DEBATE ON THE
IMPLAUSIBILITY OF AN AFTER-LIFE

I have never believed in a life after death even when I was a Christian fellow traveller, nor do I believe in the existence of a soul. I dislike the thought of dying as much as the next man but I prefer Marcus Aurelius's calm acceptance to Christianity's false hopes. Nevertheless, I have come this evening to the Institute of Psychiatry at the Maudsley Hospital in South London to hear four scientists debate the motion that 'This house believes that modern neuroscience has demonstrated the implausibility of an after life.'

I am drawn here by the fact that three of the main speakers are scientists I have already met on my journey. The atheists, Peter Atkins and Lewis Wolpert are proposing the motion and John Polkinghorne, the mathematical physicist who is also an Anglican priest is opposing. The lecture theatre is crowded with staff and students from the Institute and from King's College Hospital across the road. I don't think an audience of this calibre will have much truck with the idea of life after death and after hearing the atheists put their case I shall not be surprised if the motion is carried by a large majority. Belief in an after life, Peter Atkins tells the audience, is a manifestation of our inability to come to terms with our annihilation. We long to survive but there is not a jot of evidence that we will.

The atheists' case is familiar but I am curious to know how John Polkinghorne, the master of the fighting retreat, will deploy his argument. He starts by recognising that evolution has rendered untenable the traditional Christian belief that there is a soul separate from the body which will survive death and provide the continuity between this life and the next. Our evolution can be traced back two billion years through the simplest life forms to bacteria, so unless God added a soul at a much later stage in the evolutionary process, Christians will have to think again. What Polkinghorne proposes is that instead of a soul, continuity between this life and the next may be provided by each individual's 'information-bearing pattern' that will be held in God's memory after death and then re-embodied by God in some new environment of His choosing. To his puzzled listeners he explains that the information-bearing pattern is the 'real me', that ensures continuity between childhood and adulthood despite the fact that the atoms that make up our bodies are forever being replaced.

Once again, as I did when we met in Cambridge, I admire John Polkinghorne's fertile mind and his refusal as a Christian to admit defeat. He is supported by Dr Sean Spence, the neuroscientist, who warns us that science has its limitations and can tell us nothing that contradicts the idea of an after-life. Nor can science prove or disprove near-death experiences any more that a brain-scan can discover whether someone is in love so that strictly speaking the audience is bound to oppose the motion as neuroscience cannot demonstrate the plausibility or the implausibility of an after-life.

He speaks well but when the debate is thrown open to the house it is clear that the vote is going to be a referendum on the after-life not on what neuroscience can or cannot prove and I doubt whether this hard-headed audience has been persuaded to abandon reason and common sense. But I am wrong. When the vote is taken, John Polkinghorne and Sean Spence win hands down. Seventy people, including myself, vote for the motion and one hundred and fifty vote against. By a majority of two to one, the atheists have been defeated and those who want to keep alive the possibility of a life after death have won.

On the bus back to Waterloo, through Brixton and Camberwell where many shops are still open at this late hour, I try without success to explain the resounding defeat of the motion by an audience whose choice of career suggests that they base their decisions on reason rather than wishful thinking. Does the vote have any bearing on whether I should consider the possibility of God's existence? I could regard it as further evidence that intelligent people are just as prone to self-deception as anyone else but belief in an after life is so intimately linked with belief in God I cannot ignore the vote altogether.

I ask myself whether I have been given any reason to believe in a life after death but I can think of none. Nothing in the debate persuaded me, on the contrary the fact that a Christian and scientist of John Polkinghorne's ability was reduced to proposing 'an information bearing pattern' as a substitute for the discredited soul, suggested to me how weak the case for an after life must be. It is possible that talk of near-death experiences encouraged the audience to abandon reason, particularly when a senior doctor spoke eloquently about his dying patients telling him that they could see a bright light and a loved one, who was already dead, coming to welcome them but to regard these things as evidence for survival is to endorse the unscientific world of the paranormal.

From the start of my journey I have been reluctant to look into the claims of the paranormal but now I think I shall have to do so, at least in relation to near-death experiences. In the meantime, the debate has made me reflect on my own attitude to dying and death. I have had cancer in the form of a malignant melanoma which has recurred once and may recur again. I share the common desire that dying should be as painless as possible and that if my mind has gone, I shall not be kept alive for the sake of it. The classical ideal, <u>felix opportunitate mortis</u>, was to die just in time before the mind and body deteriorated. As I believe death will be the end, I view its approach without enthusiasm but with as much of Marcus Aurelius's stoicism as I can muster, though I find myself oscillating between his philosophical, 'If it is time to go, leave willingly', and Dylan Thomas's 'Rage, rage against the dying of the light.' Instead of the comforting thought of life after death, I like to think about life going on without me. The world existed for billions of years before I was conceived and will do the same after my death, and although I shall not be here, my genes will live on, initially in our children and grandchildren and then in heaven knows how many generations until the sun cools and the human race disappears. We shall all have been part of the human adventure and that should be consolation enough.

I do not begrudge those who believe in an after life their consolation but I think they would be unwise to base their hopes on reports of near-death experiences. The typical near-death experience occurs when the individual 'comes back to life' after being thought to be clinically dead. The 'returning' individual reports seeing a tunnel leading towards a figure of light and having sensations of warmth and welcome, a very similar experience to that reported by the doctor in the debate only in his cases the individuals were conscious. Individuals who were unconscious, typically in the operating theatre, also report that they seem to float above their own body.

Is this evidence of survival after death and if so, does it strengthen the odds on God's existence? These questions have brought me to the Society of Psychical Research which was founded in 1882 to examine in a scientific spirit 'those faculties of man, real or supposed, which appear to be inexplicable on any generally recognised hypothesis.' The Society's office is well placed above a firm of funeral furnishers in a quiet street off the Cromwell Road in West London and its library, which is at the back of the building, is stocked with works on every aspect of the paranormal from thought transference and mediumship to reincarnation events of the sort that interested Andrew Huxley.

Mainstream scientists do not accept psychical research because it cannot be tested in the laboratory and does not obey the rules of natural science but they are not the only sceptics. Christian theologians, too, are cautious or in some cases, dismissive. Even though near-death experiences are treated by some theologians with greater respect than other paranormal phenomena, they got short shrift from the great

Roman Catholic theologian, Hans Kung, who said of them, 'What then do these experiences of dying imply for life after death? To put it briefly, nothing.'

Near-death experiences are not evidence for an after life for the simple reason that those who have the experience were never dead. From my reading in the Society's library, I gather that doctors and psychologists regard near-death experiences as the natural reaction of the dying brain or perhaps more accurately, of the brain that thinks it is dying. That the experiences have a profound affect on the individual is to be expected; even convinced atheists may think again. The philosopher, A.J. Ayer, who was, like Richard Dawkins, the most prominent atheist of his day, had a near-death experience when he was critically ill with pneumonia. Asked whether this had changed his opinion that death would be the end, he replied: 'My recent experiences have slightly weakened my conviction that my genuine death will be the end of me though I continue to hope that it will.'

As I feared it would be, the paranormal is a cul-de-sac and I shall find no reason here to consider seriously the possible existence of God. What little I have learnt about the Society for Psychical Research persuades me that they are not cranks and genuinely attempt to examine paranormal claims in a scientific spirit but when I read in their Journal a careful analysis of mediumship or of a child's inexplicable knowledge of the life of a dead stranger, my reaction is to ask 'So what?'. Either the evidence is trickery or science will sooner or later demonstrate that what appeared to be paranormal can be explained by the laws of nature.

What science cannot explain is why anything exists at all and it is this philosophical question not hope of an after life that motivates my desire to discover what I really believe. I could never take seriously a God who promised me eternal life because I would not believe him. Does that rule me out as a candidate for Christianity or is a belief in a life after death now an optional extra? My impression is that the Christians I have met on this journey expect death to be the end but would be reluctant to preach that message from the pulpit. They are not being dishonest or hypocritical just sensitive to the fact that the Church as an institution and the laity are not yet ready to abandon belief in an after life. From my point of view, speculation about a life after death is a red herring and I shall not waste may more time on it.

13

IN WHICH I MEET A FORMER NUN
WHO HAS BECOME AN AUTHORITY ON
THE WORLD'S RELIGIONS

Karen Armstrong's house is a short walk from the Angel Underground Station in North London. I am here for a specific purpose. I know from Karen's writing that, having once been a Roman Catholic nun, she now understands religion in a different way, not as assent to propositions about a metaphysical God but as a commitment to the Golden Rule that lies at the heart of all the great world religions. I am hoping that from her unique standpoint of Christian faith and profound insight into the other world religions she can help me sort out my confused ideas about the meaning of the word God. I have had great difficulty understanding what the believers and non-believers I have met mean when they use the word. Is God a supernatural being, the subject of metaphysical speculation or 'the deepest interiority of our being'? When I asked Martin Rees why he was not an atheist, he replied, 'What God would I not believe in'? And I can see that there is a danger that I shall reach the end of my journey with no clear idea of what God I am accepting or rejecting. We talk in a quiet restaurant away from the traffic and bustle of Upper Street and I ask her what she understands by the Golden Rule.

'Do not do unto others as you would not have done unto you,' she replies. 'Confucius taught that Golden Rule five hundred years before Christ. The Buddha taught it, Jesus taught it and it is what underlies the teaching of the Qur'an.'

'And of Judaism?'

'Yes. Rabbi Hillet, an older contemporary of Jesus, told a group of pagans who wanted him to recite the whole of Jewish teaching: "That which is hateful to you, do not to your neighbour. That is the Torah. The rest is commentary. Go and study it."'

The words of Mahatma Gandhi come to mind. 'There is one true and perfect religion but it becomes many as it passes through the human medium.' But is the Golden Rule a religion or just a philosophy of life that can be extracted from any of the great religions and can be bolted onto agnosticism or atheism? I put it to Karen that in her commitment to the Golden Rule, there is no role for God.

'Not in our traditional Western sense of God,' she says. 'But the West has always had a reductive and too rationalistic a view of the divine, which is one of the underlying reasons for the schism with the Greek Orthodox Church. The other monotheistic traditions - Judaism, Orthodox Christianity and Islam have all developed more "Buddhist" style views of the divine and the sacred. God isn't necessarily to be considered a person with whom we have a relationship. The Hindus, for example, would find it impossible to speak to Brahman, because Brahman is the core of their being: it would be like talking to oneself, and you can certainly see God like that too. Nearly all the great mystics of the monotheistic traditions have insisted that God is not simply transcendent; we also find the divine in others and within ourselves. This is sound Christian doctrine. In this sense we are all incarnations of the divine. This was made clear by the great Sufi philosopher Muid ad Din Ibn al Arabi, who said that every single person who had been born into the world is a unique and unrepeatable revelation of the divine, and incarnation of one of God's hidden names'.

I don't think Timothy Radcliffe would disagree with that though he would add that what is divine in each one of us is our capacity for unpossessive love, for that unDarwinian selflessness that Dawkins says is unprecedented in four billion years of evolution but is a product of evolution nevertheless.

The thought prompts me to tell Karen that Dawkins and I agreed that if we saw a man beating a child with a stick on the road outside, we would go out to stop him and that this would have nothing to do with whether or not we believed in God.

'A third century Chinese philosopher whose Latinised name was Mencius drew attention to that basic human impulse long ago,' Karen says. 'He pointed out that if you see a child about to fall into a well, you rush to save it with no calculation of the possible benefits such as the gratitude of the parents or the praise of your neighbours. His point was that altruism is built into our human nature, and that we must cultivate it assiduously - then we would experience the divine, and, in a sense, become divine ourselves. "Believing in God" is a very simplistic idea of faith, by the way. Most of the traditions teach that the disciplined practice of compassion, day by day, hour by hour, gives us an experience of transcendence that some have called "God" and others Nirvana, Brahman or the Dao. The problem is that people first learn about "God" when they are small children, at about the same time as they hear about Santa Claus. Their ideas about Santa change over the years, but their ideas about God, which are necessarily infantile, don't.'

'If believing in God is a very simplistic idea of faith, what about the propositions in the Creed to which as a Roman Catholic you must have assented many times?'

'The creedal propositions each contain a kernel of spiritual insight that goes far beyond their literal plain sense,' Karen replies, 'but as propositions they are irrelevant to faith because faith is not belief. To equate faith with believing certain ideas is a very eccentric notion in the history of religion, and has been current only in the West since the Enlightenment. The word "credo" probably comes from co do: I give my heart. And the Middle English beleven meant "to love," not to suspend judgment about intellectual matters. None of the other great traditions regard faith in this way. The Qur'an calls this kind of compulsory theology jannah: self-indulgent guess work about unverifiable matters, which makes people quarrelsome and sectarian. None of the major world faiths put any emphasis on "believing things". Religion is not about thinking things, but about doing things - such as putting the Golden Rule into practice, day by day, hour by hour, minute by minute - that change you at a profound level. Metaphysical speculation is interesting but unless it leads to compassionate action it is irrelevant to the project of faith. Faith is not a matter of suspending disbelief, but assiduously cultivating an attitude of trust (as when we say that we have faith in a person or idea) that against all the depressing evidence to the contrary, life has some ultimate meaning and value. But all the faiths including Christianity, insist that that "meaning" is transcendent and ineffable. It cannot be defined, any more than you can "define" the meaning of a late Beethoven quartet, which also gives you intimations of ultimate meaning.'

Not for the first time on this journey, I am out of my depth when someone talks about life having 'ultimate meaning.' What in that context does 'meaning' mean? The Golden Rule I do understand but is Karen saying that the Golden Rule is synonymous with religion?

'All the major faiths agree that the Golden Rule is religion,' she says. 'As Rabbi Hillel said: everything else is only "commentary." Confucius was the first person to insist that religion is simply altruism and he was the first to propound the Golden Rule, which, he said, must be practised "all day and every day." And that gives you a transcendent experience. You, John, seem stuck in the supernaturalist notion of the divine, but not all faiths have a clear concept of the supernatural. Buddhism doesn't; the Chinese would see the divine as inseparable from the natural. You also have a purely notional view of religion, which you expect to understand immediately in the same way as you understand any logical or rational proposition, in a simple act of cognition. But religious "truth" is akin to the insights of art: it can take years to cultivate an aesthetic understanding of painting, poetry or music. At first sight, a painting by Picasso can seem opaque and incomprehensible; it is only after you have made a serious effort to accommodate your ideas with the "language" of the artist, divesting your own ideas of what a picture ought to be, that you begin to see what an artist like Picasso is doing. Without this kind of assiduous cultivation, the truths of religion make no sense either. Religion is a kind of ethical aesthetic. The only way we can get a sense of what we call God is to do it, to live a compassionate life. That is the conclusion of nearly every major religious sage and thinker. From Confucius, the Upanishads, Mahavira, Buddha, the Hebrew Prophets, Hillel, Muhammad, Jesus on. None of these people is interested in the kind of metaphysical speculation about God that you seem to equate with "religion."'

I ask, 'Is there any reason why an agnostic or an atheist should not be just as capable of living by the Golden Rule, of recognising what is unique and precious in other people?'

'No, of course not. I am absolutely clear about that. Having the correct theology (which is what you seem to mean by "religion") is not a prerequisite for the compassionate life or from the enlightenment that comes with it. But the religious traditions do have a storehouse of wisdom that has been acquired over the ages, with great creativity and painstaking discipline, and can thus help those of us who simply don't have time to invent the wheel, and find out all these things from scratch.'

'But you don't belong to any religious tradition?'

'Not at the moment. I am still "convalescent," after a difficult religious experience in youth. I recovered my enthusiasm for the religious quest by the study of different religious traditions and found that there was a lot that I could relate to - including the fact that they all insist that our ideas about God or Nirvana and so on bear no relation at all to the ineffable reality itself that cannot be defined. I do not see any one of these faith traditions as superior to any of the others. So I would find it difficult - at present - to confine myself to a single creed. All the traditions are profoundly at one about the matters that I have tried to outline to you, but each has its special genius and each its particular failings. I don't think it matters what you believe: if your belief makes you kind and respectful of others, it is good religion; if it makes you belligerent and intolerant, it is not good religion, however firm your beliefs. And that goes for people with secularist beliefs too. In all the major traditions, practical compassion is the test of good spiritual practice and ideas.'

I suggest that she has found her way via Roman Catholicism and a scholarly study of other faiths to a religion in which God is just a word that means the goal of selflessness and empathy with others towards which we should direct our lives.

'Not exactly: "God" is certainly a word, which, like every word, points beyond itself to a reality that transcends it. About difficult and elusive matters, words are always unsatisfactory - that is a major theme of both literature and religion. And God is a very unsatisfactory word, especially if it makes you imagine that it points to a concrete object. The major theologians insist that God is not another being; that it is more accurate to say that God does not exist, because our notion of existence is too limited to apply to God, who does not exist like a computer and is not even an unseen reality like the atom, but more like the intuitions of art. But,the religions have concluded, selflessness and compassion can give you intimations of transcendence that some have called God, others Nirvana, Brahman or the Dao. No amount of metaphysical speculation can prove God: all intelligent theologians are at one about that. The only way to approach it is by doing religion not by talking about it'.

I feel like an amateur boxer who has gone ten rounds with a professional and is not sure what lessons he has learnt. This is what I think Karen is saying.

Religion is practical compassion, the cultivation of the altruism that is built into our human nature. By practicing, day by day, the selflessness that puts others at the centre of our world, we become aware of the divine in ourselves and in other people. This awareness, that some have called God, cannot be proved or defined or put into words. It can only be experienced. It seems that for Karen the use of the word God is an optional, take it or leave it, way of referring to 'the intimations of transcendence' that result from a life dedicated to selflessness and compassion. As I head back to the Angel, I am thinking that everyone's attempts to understand the world would be made a lot easier if we banned the word God altogether and concentrated on the idea of religion as a practical compassion, the cultivation of the altruism that is built into our human nature.

14

IN WHICH I TRY TO UNDERSTAND THE NATURE OF ST TERESA'S RELIGIOUS EXPERIENCES

The idea of religion as practical compassion rather than belief in a supernatural God makes me all the more curious about the religious experiences of St. Teresa of Avila. If such an intelligent and able person believed that she had direct encounters with God, was she deluding herself or is there something in the idea of a supernatural God after all?

I tread carefully because however much I read about mysticism, I do not really understand what is going on but the great thing about Saint Teresa is that she did not understand either and said so. I doubt whether anyone has reflected on religious experience with such intellectual honesty as she did. On the ultimate religious experience of union with God, she confessed that 'the understanding, if it understands, does not know how it understands.' This is why she is, for me, the key witness on religious experience. She is too perceptive, too aware of the limits of language, too down to earth and has too keen a sense of humour, to be dismissed as deluded or hysterical.

Teresa Sanchez de Cepeda Y Ahumada was born in Avila on 28th March 1515, the third child of the second marriage of Don Alonso, a Spanish nobleman who hid the fact that his father was Jewish so successfully that Teresa's biographers knew nothing of this until 1947. Teresa was born at the start of Spain's Golden Century when her country achieved the height of its power and influence. This was the Spain of Cervantes and Lope de Vega, of universities that led the intellectual life of Europe but it was also the Spain of the Inquisition, of religious fanaticism and racial intolerance.

At the age of twenty-one, Teresa made her own decision, against her father's wishes, to enter the Carmelite Convent of the Incarnation outside the walls of Avila. For the next nineteen years, her life as a nun, though outwardly uneventful, was restless and unhappy because she was troubled by doubts and by a sense of failure. She found it so hard to pray that she almost gave up trying. 'Whenever I entered the oratory,' she wrote, 'I used to feel so depressed that I had to summon up all my courage to make myself pray at all.'

Exactly when the turning point in her spiritual life occurred is not clear but it was probably in 1555 when she was forty and discovered the writings of St. Augustine recently translated into Spanish. Augustine's Confessions seemed to reflect her own experience and helped her to dispel the spiritual indifference that had made her religious life such a struggle against apathy. To help herself to pray, she developed a programme that enabled her to move through different states of consciousness away from the world and towards union with God, and it was in the third stage of these mystical prayers, which she described as a state of ecstasy, that her most striking religious experiences occurred. They took the form of seeing visions of Christ and hearing the voice of God speaking to her (her 'divine locutions').

Visions and voices occur in some forms of mental disorder but Saint Teresa's calm analysis and evaluation of her visions and voices could not have been made by a mentally disordered person. She was very suspicious of those religious experiences in which she thought she saw someone and only really had confidence in those in which she had an inner feeling of a presence. The ones she believed to be authentic were therefore the ones she found most difficult to explain. The way she tries to explain a vision to her Jesuit confessor, Father Baltason Alvarez, seems to me exactly how a sane person would respond to the challenge of describing a mystical experience.

Teresa describes this vision in these words:

I was at prayer on the festival of the glorious St. Peter when I saw Christ at my side, or, to put it better, I was conscious of Him for neither with the eyes of the body nor with those of the soul did I see anything. I thought He was quite close to me and I saw that it was He who, as I thought, was speaking to me. Being completely ignorant that visions of this kind could occur, I was at first very much afraid, and did nothing but weep, though, as soon as He addressed a single word to me to reassure me, I became quiet again, as I had been before, and was quite happy and free from fear.'

Alvarez was cautiously sceptical. The Inquisition was on the look out for false mystics. In what form had she seen Christ? Teresa replied that she had not seen Him at all. Then how did she know it was Christ? Teresa said she did not know how but she knew that He was beside her. She tried a number of comparisons to convince Alvarez – it was like being blind and knowing that someone else was in the room – until she suggested a comparison that Alvarez appears to have grasped, no doubt because it appealed to a Jesuit's intellectual cast of mind. Knowing that Christ was present in a vision, she suggested, was like finding oneself in possession of all knowledge without having learned the alphabet.

Whatever explanations there may be for St. Teresa's religious experiences, mental disorder is not one of them. The most likely explanation is also the most obvious. Mystical experiences are not confined to Christianity. Saint Teresa's techniques for detaching herself from all distracting images and thoughts in order to reach a different state of consciousness, would have found a parallel in the religious traditions of Islam, Hinduism and Buddhism but while the techniques may have been similar the visions were different. A Hindu in a state of ecstasy would not have had a vision of Jesus Christ because the vision must take its origin from an image already in the mind. Christian mystics' visions of the crucifixion often corresponded in their detail not to the actual facts of the crucifixion but the famous paintings of the subject. Saint Teresa, having reached a state of ecstasy, was bound to have mystical experiences that reflected her religious preoccupations. It is even possible to trace the origin of her most celebrated religious experience to a German Benedictine nun of the thirteenth century.

Bernini's famous sculpture in the Church of Santa Maria della Vittoria in Rome captures the moment when Saint Teresa in a state of ecstasy had a vision of an angel who pierced her heart several times with a golden spear but this vision did not come to Saint Teresa out of the blue. She had read in Spanish an account of the great German mystic, Sister Gertrude, who had a vision of Christ piercing her heart with a triple-pointed arrow. Saint Teresa was not guilty of plagiarism, it is just that the famous religious experience had its origin in an image already on her mind.

Does it follow that there was nothing supernatural about Saint Teresa's religious experiences? I think it does but if I met Saint Teresa and she told me about her visions and voices, I would not advise her to see a psychiatrist. Her religious experiences do not require a psychological or a supernatural explanation. They were normal in the sense that they are what you would expect when a sane and intensely religious person achieves altered states of consciousness through mystical prayer. Down to earth as ever, Saint Teresa did not think her visions were important in themselves; they only had value if they led to a greater love of God and a more perfect obedience to His will. It was the effect of her visions on her life that mattered.

A historian of Spain's Golden Century with no religious axe to grind described Saint Teresa as 'one of the greatest women in history and certainly the greatest woman in Spain's literary history,' and the more I know about her life, the more I share his opinion, but while I admire her reform of the Carmelite Order in the face of fierce opposition, particularly male opposition, and the simplicity and frankness of her writing about mysticism, I am sure that her visions and voices, her raptures and levitations and her transverberations of the heart were part of an earthly reality not a heavenly one.

15

IN WHICH I MEET THE FORMER
BISHOP OF EDINBURGH WHO
IS IN NOBODY'S CAMP

I have come to Edinburgh to re-visit agnosticism. Richard Hollo-way was Bishop of Edinburgh from 1986 to 2000. He still lives in the city and we meet at his house in Morningside. He has described himself as a 'post-Christian', even on one occasion as a 'recovering Christian' as though Christianity was a form of addiction. He attends church and takes part in the services while no longer believing that the religious language he is using refers to a real God. He does not recognise the divinity of Jesus Christ yet rejects the term 'agnostic' because that implies neutrality and he prefers to define his position as 'committed unknowing.' Disputes about the existence of God he regards as pointless because that question is intrinsically and endur-ingly unknowable. I am not at all surprised when he adds that he admires both Dr Rowan Williams, the Archbishop of Canterbury and Richard Dawkins, with whom he shared a platform at the Edinburgh Book Festival. The former Bishop of Edinburgh is in nobody's camp.

For a wandering agnostic who leans towards atheism one day and theism the next this sounds almost too good to be true. Is 'post-Christian committed unknowing' where I belong? I have never been addicted to Christianity, even the term post-Christian would exaggerate my involvement, and I prefer Umberto Eco's 'restless incredulity' to 'committed unknowing' but there is much in Rich-ard Holloway's grown-up attitude to religion that I find attractive though I cannot understand why a recovering Christian wants to go to church. Isn't that rather like a recovering alcoholic popping into the pub?

'The Christian narrative, from Genesis to the gospels, still has meaning and value for me,' he says, 'Do you know Wittgenstein?'

I have been here before but to my relief, Richard Holloway is easier to follow than Don Cupitt.. What he has taken from Wittgenstein is the idea that religious language can still have meaning even though it is not speaking about a real God.

'For an atheist, there is no God so religious language is meaningless. For Christians, religious language is given meaning by their belief that God is a supernatural reality. I do not believe that God is a supernatural reality but I still value religious language because it is the way we tell ourselves the narrative of our search for a meaning. The supernatural element in Christianity may be myth but the myth is important, it still has value.'

It sounds as though he has taken the same route as Don Cupitt away from supernatural religion but unlike Cupitt he has not tried to find a new job for the redundant word 'God', indeed he hardly uses the word God at all. His commitment is to searching for a meaning to human existence.

'What sort of meaning are we talking about?'

His answer is unexpectedly precise.

'We should identify the things that are really precious to human flourishing and defend them against the odds.'

I may be reading too much into what he says but I hear once again an echo of Timothy Radcliffe's unpossessive love and of Richard Dawkins unDarwinian selflessness. Is it possible that a former Master of the Dominican Order, a former Protestant bishop who has left supernatural religion far behind and a leading atheist are all identifying our capacity for selflessness as the one thing that might give meaning to human existence?

I ask Richard Holloway how he got on with Dawkins when they shared a platform at the book festival. The common ground apparently was that they both recognised that this capacity for selflessness makes humanity an oddity, a 'singularity' in evolution. Dawkins is sure that however unDarwinian human selflessness may be it is still a product of blind evolution not the creation of an intelligence behind the universe but for Timothy Radcliffe the human capacity for unpossessive love that makes sense of our existence is not something that belongs in the realm of science at all.

Richard Holloway, the post-Christian, accepts that the human potential for selflessness is a product of blind evolution but he believes we should live our lives as though it wasn't, as though love really is the purpose of the Universe as so many of the Christians I have met believe.

Let me get this right. There is no God so human life has no meaning or purpose beyond itself but we can give it meaning by punching above our weight morally or, if that metaphor is not helpful, by realising our potential to be less self-centered than we usually are. Isn't that what Karen Armstrong was saying about cultivating the altruism that is built into our human nature? But is it possible for us to live lives of unDarwinian selflessness without the help of religion?

Richard Holloway believes that it is because our moral values are not targets set by God, they are something we have created ourselves, they have evolved with our experience and they are still evolving. 'Look at the way our attitude to the role of women, to sexual orientation and to racial difference have changed over the last fifty years.' He also sees a reason to hope that we can stand on our own feet morally in the fact that we have evolved tendencies to co-operate as well as to compete with one another.

He is an optimist. I am more pessimistic about human nature and think there must be some doubt whether we can live up to the ideal of unDarwinian selflessness without someone or something to bring out the best in us. That is not an argument for believing in the existence of God; it is just a reminder that in the past we let the promise of heaven and the fear of hell underwrite our moral values. When Pope John Paul 11 was asked whether hell still exists, he made an interesting distinction between belief in hell, which had declined, and faith in God 'as Supreme Justice' which had not. 'The expectation remains' he said, 'that there is Someone who, in the end, will be able to speak the truth about the good and evil that man does, Someone able to reward the good and punish the bad ... Is not hell in a certain sense the ultimate safeguard of man's moral conscience?'

It is all very well for Richard Dawkins to say that we should encourage human superniceness, by taking Jesus, stripped of the supernatural nonsense, as our role model and for Don Cupitt to say that the man Jesus is the embodiment of his religious ideal, but can Jesus, the man, the role-model, be the ultimate safeguard of our moral conscience? Once we remove God as 'Supreme Justice' we are on our own when it comes to safeguarding our moral values. I do not believe that the atrocities committed by the atheistic regimes of Hitler, Stalin and Pol Pot, demonstrate the dangers of going it alone morally, equally terrible cruelties were committed in the name of God, but all these cruelties show how close we have always lived and still live to the frontier with barbarism.

Richard Holloway recognises this but he remains optimistic not least because evolution produces individuals who have the courage to challenge power. He is fascinated by this evolutionary phenomenon of which, he suggests, Jesus is the supreme example. As long as there are people who will challenge power, we will be able to safeguard our moral values and to defend those things that are precious to human flourishing.

If I had to use one word to characterise Richard Holloway's post-Christian attitude to life it would be 'defiance' – defiance of power, defiance of an indifferent universe, defiance of pessimism, defiance of our selfish egoism. He does not believe in God but he does believe in the future of a global community that is capable without divine help of defending those moral values that underpin our common humanity. He knows death will be the end but that is not a reason to despair. On the contrary, 'we should live the fleeting day with passion and, when the night comes, depart from it with grace.'

I follow my usual routine and, back in the city centre, find a coffee shop on Prince's Street where I can reflect on our conversation and remember the questions I forgot to ask. There is so much about Richard Holloway's 'committed unknowing' I feel at home with, I am angry with myself for doubting whether this is where I belong. But the doubt persists and it is this. If Richard does not believe in God or in a life after death, what is there left to be unknowing about?

This question is so fundamental to my understanding of his position that I include here the answer he gave when I asked him to look through the draft of this chapter.

'My answer is that I am in a state of unknowing about the ultimate nature of the universe, why it is rather than isn't, and whether it has any kind of coherent purpose within itself. There is an enduring mystery about the sheer fact of the universe. Some say they know it has no meaning, others say they know its meaning lies in its having been created by a god. For me, it is unknowable. But there may be something hinted at as to its nature by the important emphasis meaning and purpose have for us. That said, you are right to sum up my position as defiance, though I'd prefer love and defiance. Even if it means nothing, is brutally indifferent to joy and love and beauty, that does not mean that we have to go with its grain: we can choose to go against it, choose to defy it, choose to live purpose into it. That's enough for me.'

In the bright winter sunshine I walk from the coffee shop to the Royal Scot Club where Father Jack Mahoney is giving us lunch. How typical of the Jesuits that they should have told Jack, 'You'll need a club', when he was appointed to an academic post at the university. Jack is a friend of long-standing – he taught my wife moral theology when he was Principal of Heythrop College in the 1970s – and he was the first person I consulted when I decided to make this journey. He is in the great Jesuit tradition of godliness, worldliness and intellectual rigour – he effectively created business ethics as a serious academic study in Britain when he was Professor at the London Business School – and I value his advice above all others on whether I should continue my journey or accept the destination I know I am approaching. So we settle down after lunch in the club library, surrounded by books on the history of Scottish regiments, and I put the question to him, 'How do I know when to stop?'

Jack suggests an analogy with academic research; this subject of all subjects is open-ended but sooner or later I will have to finish and if I think I am approaching a destination, then this is a good time to write up my conclusions and hand in my dissertation. It need not be my last word on the subject, just a snapshot of what I believe now. 'You will probably find,' he adds, 'that as one journey ends, another begins.'

16

IN WHICH I MEET A BENEDICTINE NUN WHO HAS LIVED AS A HERMIT AND TRANSLATED ST. AUGUSTINE'S 'CONFESSIONS'

Dark clouds and heavy showers have accompanied us across the Cotswolds but when we drop down into the Vale of Evesham the clouds clear and sunlight glistens on the wet grass and the rows of apple trees in blossom. Our destination is the Benedictine monastery of Stanbrook Abbey between Worcester and the Malvern hills. I want to make one last attempt to understand what God means to someone who has had a lifelong relationship with Him, and I am pinning my hopes on a nun who until recently lived the solitary life of a hermit, praying, growing vegetables and translating The Confessions of St. Augustine from late Latin into English.

Sister Maria Boulding joined the Benedictine Order in 1947 at the age of eighteen and has been at Stanbrook Abbey ever since. When she enters by the frosted glass door that separates the visitor's room from the enclosure, I am surprised that she looks so young and say, 'In the outside world I would have made a foolish, flattering comment.' She smiles. 'But you won't will you?' She is wearing the traditional black habit of the Benedictines.

I ask about the origin of her interest in St. Augustine. When she came to Stanbrook fifty-eight years ago there were already a number of nuns with a scholarly interest in the early Church fathers. After Vatican II much translation into English was needed for readings in the liturgy, and various Stanbrook nuns shared in this work, including Sister Maria. Later she worked for many years for a publishing institute specialising in the works of St Augustine. Her translation of St. Augustine's <u>Confessions</u> is widely read and admired and she is currently involved in a new translation of the liturgy into English, a work that takes her to meetings abroad, in Rome and the United States.

'Do hermits travel?'

She lived as a hermit for twenty years, supported by her community. Now living back in the monastery, her articulate, friendly, good-humoured personality, is curiously at odds with my idea of a hermit.

St. Teresa of Avila is still on my mind so I ask whether religious experience is an important part of faith.

'St Teresa's central teaching on faith and prayer is always valid, a gift to the Church and to all who pray. But if by religious experience you mean such phenomena as visions and ecstasies, the answer is No. St Teresa would be the first to say that religious experiences of that sort are not essential to faith, they are peripheral, they prove nothing either way.'

'Is it possible to describe what it means to have faith, to have a relationship with God?'

'Words always betray us,' Sister Maria replies, 'and the metaphors we use to talk about God are never more than partially true because they are coined by the human mind. One way I know I have a relationship with God in faith is when I am unexpectedly aware of the coherence of everything, aware that in spite of so much evidence to the contrary, reality is good.'

'When you are at prayer?'

'Not necessarily. It is much more likely to happen when I am doing the washing up but especially when I am with other people.'

'I am trying to pin down God's role in the relationship.'

'If you meet a really holy person, he makes you feel a whole lot better about yourself, that you are not inferior but really loved, and when that happens, you know intuitively that the better person he sees in you is also what is truest about you. Does that make sense? This encounter with holiness is a pointer to the nature of our relationship with God. God knows us better than anyone and loves us better than anyone and he sees in us what we are really capable of being, and we, in our heart of hearts, know that his high hopes of us are also what is truest about us.'

I remember what a boost it was if someone I admired thought more highly of me than I deserved but how can God do that if I am not persuaded of his existence? There is a prayer which begins, 'O gracious and holy father give us wisdom to perceive thee ...' but if I am ever going to perceive God it will have to be without his help. Does that make sense? If I try to explain this to Sister Maria, she may think I am inventing difficulties to protect my agnosticism but for me the difficulty is as real as awareness of God is real for her. Born into a Catholic family, she imbibed Christianity from the earliest years and has 'never really not believed in God.' I am not suggesting that faith came easily but that she has always been able to interpret reality in the context of her profound conviction that God is there. Part of me is envious, as I might be of someone who was born with an outstanding talent I did not possess, and part of me accepts that some people have to come to terms with reality in their own way.

When I say something along these lines, Sister Maria quotes Pascal, 'Comfort yourself, you would not seek me if you had not found me.' Of genuine seekers that may be true but I did not start this journey with the working assumption that there was a God to find, on the contrary, and one of the reasons for my scepticism was that I could not take seriously all those propositions in the creed about the resurrection of the body and the life everlasting.

'Faith is not about believing certain propositions,' Sister Maria says. 'Faith is a gift from God, given because he wants us to have a direct relationship with himself.'

'Then why bother with the propositions?'

'Because we need them. Our faith doesn't exist in isolation, we are part of a great tradition and the propositions that we hold in common are a vital element in that tradition, ensuring that every member of the church, from the most humble to the most powerful, shares the same fundamental beliefs.'

'But are the propositions true?'

'They are inadequate but not untrue. In human language they fall far short but they are still for us an open window onto the truth.'

'What is the truth about the resurrection?'

'We are not talking about resuscitating a corpse, but neither is the resurrection just a metaphor for some purely spiritual event. Christ is truly risen in a bodily sense: his human body and human mind are caught up into the glory of God, as ours will be one day, with him. His resurrection is a mystery, not in the sense of an Agatha Christie thriller to which we shall discover the solution, but in the sense of an insight into the mysterious nature of God and of His relationship with His Son. Or to put it another way, the proposition about the resurrection or the incarnation is a torch that we hold to guide us into the darkness, or a survival kit for the explorer into the heart of a mystery that we shall never fully understand.'

We have been talking for an hour when, at five o'clock, the Abbey bell starts to ring and behind the frosted glass shadowy figures hurry by. I assume they are hurrying to a service but Sister Maria tells me they are all heading for the television room. The bell is a signal that a new pope has been elected and the nuns want to see who it is.

A nun appears at the door to say that Vespers has been brought forward an hour. Sister Maria apologises. We shall have to continue in the morning. In the monastery church, Daphne and I are the only visitors listening to the nuns singing the office and, as we leave, four nuns pass us talking excitedly, presumably on their way back to the television room, and one calls over her shoulder 'Habemus papam'. Later, we learn that the new pope is Cardinal Ratzinger and that he is to be called Benedict XV1.

When Sister Maria and I meet again in the morning, I ask her about prayer. 'Love is in the will,' she replies, 'not in having nice feelings. You have to stick at prayer, wanting to be united with God. A lot of it may be boredom, trying to get started, trying to stay focused, trying to stay awake, having a sense of failure all the time. A great deal of prayer is not being able to pray.'

'But sometimes it works?'

'Yes, after a long time usually. I cannot capture God with my thought or feeling; I have to make myself available to him.' Then echoing words she used at the start of our discussion yesterday, she adds, 'I become aware of a reality that is not capturable, not definable.'

'Which you call God?'

'Yes.'

'And that is nothing to do with mysticism?'

'No. Spirituality not mysticism.'

'Can we talk about spirituality which is a word I have never understood. A dictionary definition is 'an instinct for religion' and I remember Basil Hume saying that man is religious by nature but I am not. I have no instinct for religion.'

'Like everyone else, you have a hunger for the truth.'

'But that is not spirituality.'

'It is one of the things that gives our life a spiritual dimension. Above all, we long for happiness and love but we know that earthly pleasures do not satisfy and do not last – death puts an end to them – so in this life we are restless and discontented. What is spiritual about our nature arises from our discontent with the human condition and our realisation that we were made for something beyond.'

Beyond? Beyond what? Beyond where? In my understanding of reality there is no beyond. If spirituality is what enables us to believe in a world beyond the world of space and time, then it is a talent that I lack.

I have the same sense of approaching the border between scepticism and belief and finding the road is blocked as I had when I was talking with Timothy Radcliffe. Once again I have encountered the real thing, a faith to die for, and in so far as I have understood it, I can recognise its appeal but it is on the other side of the border and there is no way across that I can take without compromising my integrity.

I am reluctant to leave Sister Maria, however, without trying to find some common ground and I recall the questions that the agnostic, Umberto Eco, put to the Catholic Cardinal, Carlo Maria Martini, in their first exchange of letters:

'Is there a notion of hope (and of our responsibility to the future) that could be shared by believers and nonbelievers? What can it be based on now?'

To the second question, Sister Maria suggests an answer. 'On the fact that God has taken all the initiatives and has come in search of us.'

But I think I have an answer to the first question and I put it to Sister Maria that believers and nonbelievers can share a hope for the future of humanity based on the evolution of our capacity for unpossessive love, for unDarwinian selflessness.

'We have only survived at all' she replies, 'because self-love and self-assertion are part of our nature.' In this at least, she agrees with Richard Dawkins but she does not believe that it is evolution that makes us capable of selfless, unpossessive love. We are only capable of such love if we allow God's love to flow through us. It is God who loves unpossessively not us. On our own, we cannot overrule our innate selfishness.

For Richard Dawkins, we are born selfish but also with a capacity for unDarwinian selflessness, however seldom we put it to use. For Sister Maria, we are born selfish but only by making ourselves a conduit for God's love, are we capable of divine selflessness.

How strange. The atheist is more optimistic about human nature than the Catholic nun but Sister Maria corrects me. 'Human optimism is not the same as religious hope.'

'Then there isn't a notion of hope that believers and nonbelievers can share?'

Sister Maria hesitates before replying.

'There is a prayer we use in the Church which is "for all here present, for all your people, and for all who seek You with a sincere heart." Nobody is out in the cold.'

When it is time for me to leave, I say that I shall find it hard to write up the notes of our conversations.

'I expect you will because when two people are talking like this, more is said than the words.'

We shake hands and say goodbye and she returns to the enclosure.

When I send Sister Maria the draft of my account of our meeting, she writes in reply:

'Thinking back over our conversations, I realise that there was something vital I should have said. Faith is a gift from God. It is therefore something we need to pray for – to receive it in the first place or to deepen it if it's already given. I know what you are going to say: that if you don't believe God exists it isn't possible to pray to him. But a hypothetical prayer wouldn't compromise your integrity would it? "O God, if you exist, help me to find you."'

Approaching the border between scepticism and belief and finding the road blocked will seem a pretty unsophisticated metaphor to theologians who can't discuss God without using words with six syllables but it accurately reflects what I feel about my meeting with Sister Maria. The roadblock that stops me crossing and even considering a hypothetical prayer is my inability to conceive of the idea that there is another reality, a world beyond the physical world of space and time. But if the road was not blocked I cannot think of a guide to the country beyond I would rather have than Sister Maria Boulding because, like Timothy Radcliffe, she has given me a wonderful insight into what it means to have a relationship with God. Although she seemed to reject the idea, there must be hope that we can share.

17

IN WHICH I REACH A DESTINATION

It is nearly a year since I went to Cambridge to see Andrew Huxley and Martin Rees and, although this subject of all subjects is open-ended, I think I am as clear now as I shall ever be about what I believe and do not believe. Jack Mahoney was right. It is time to write down my conclusions. Am I an agnostic still or an atheist or a believer in some sort of God?

On that first visit to Cambridge, Martin Rees spoke of the pre-eminent mystery of why anything exists at all, and that mystery has always been my starting point when I wondered about the possibility of God. I realize that for many religious people speculation about this mystery is irrelevant and a distraction from the main business of putting their faith into practice but for me, the mystery of why anything exists at all is the only context in which it makes sense to start thinking about God.

Needless to say, the mystery re-enforces my agnosticism. The reason why anything exists at all is unknowable and always will be. In six billion years, when the sun dies and the earth becomes uninhabitable, the last intelligent creatures, as different from us as we are from protozoa, will be none the wiser.

That conclusion is easily reached but I set out on my journey to answer the more difficult, supplementary question of whether there are grounds for believing that the solution to the mystery of why anything exists at all could be something or someone we call God. I could dodge this question by saying that as the answer will never be known there is no point in speculating, an approach that would have appealed to the Buddha, but I have been dodging this question all my adult life and do not intend to do so any more. The purpose of my journey was to make up my mind.

As far as I know, there are only two ways to be convinced of God's existence, one is by religious experience and the other is by reasoned argument. Again, I am well aware that in all the major faith traditions there are people who regard trying to prove God's existence as a pointless intellectual exercise because God can only be experienced not proved but if I am going to take seriously the possibility that there is a God behind the mystery of why anything exists at all, it is with this intellectual exercise that I must start.

My intellect tells me that all ideas about God, whether God is perceived as a supernatural superbeing or as an inside job, the divine in each one of us is the product of the human imagination. God did not create us, we created him and so he cannot possibly be the explanation for why anything exists at all. To be the solution to that pre-eminent mystery, God would have to be a different reality altogether and not just the creation of the human mind. Is there any evidence that this is the case?

Before answering that question, I want to be clear what I mean by saying 'God would have to be a different reality altogether.' From St. Augustine to the medieval saints such as Teresa of Avila to Timothy Radcliffe to Karen Armstrong's insights into comparative religion, the message has been that God is not a supernatural being 'out there', God is present in all of us, closer to us than we are ourselves and so on. Frankly, I do not and probably never will understand what people mean when they talk of God in this way but whether I understand or not, is this God who is present in all of us part of our reality, part of the universe we inhabit, or a different reality altogether? Although Timothy Radcliffe speaks of God who is the deepest interiority of our being, for him and for Christians of his tradition, God is also the answer to the question of why anything exists at all and to be that God must be a different reality. When Cardinal Ratzinger was inaugurated as Pope Benedict XV1, he used these words in his homily. 'We are not some casual and meaningless product of evolution. Each one of us is the result of a thought of God. Each one of us is willed, each one of us is loved, each one of us is necessary.' God may be present in all of us but only a God who is at the same time a different reality can guarantee that we are not some casual and meaningless product of evolution.

Is there any evidence then for such a God? In my ignorance, I thought that other-worldly religious experiences might be evidence but I was wrong. However many Virgin Marys appear to malnourished asthmatic waifs in remote grottoes, the case for God as a different reality is not advanced one iota. As Sister Maria Boulding pointed out, visions and ecstasies prove nothing. But whether she realises it or not, Sister Maria Boulding is herself evidence of a type of religious experience which, from my point of view, is much more interesting. I am in no doubt whatsoever that for her there is a God who is not just a product of her imagination and that when she says,' I became aware of a reality that is not capturable, not definable,' she is not saying that she imagines God's presence. In some way that I cannot understand, God who is a different reality is present for her.

For Sister Maria Boulding, religion is not just practical compassion; it is a relationship with a God who is a different reality. Even a sceptic like myself could tell that her faith was the real thing, a faith to die for, so it was all the more frustrating to be unable to bridge the gulf between her faith and my scepticism. Her suggestion that I should pray a hypothetical prayer, 'O God, if you exist, help me to find you', could only have worked if reasoned argument had persuaded me that it was worth trying.

Sister Maria's hypothetical prayer illustrates the dilemma, the catch-22, for nonbelievers who want to understand religious faith. Only by giving God the benefit of the doubt will I discover why it is worth giving God the benefit of the doubt. Or as Sister Teresa Keswick did not say but might have done: 'Where God is concerned, the proof of the pudding is in the eating.' Even Timothy Radcliffe who understood better than anyone why I was looking for reasoned arguments, nevertheless at times in our conversations said in effect: 'If you accept that the world is God's creation, His gift, everything makes sense, everything falls into place.'

Some nonbelievers may have no difficulty taking the existence of God in trust but others, including myself, want a reason to do so; not proof of God's existence but a reasoned argument for taking the possibility of a God seriously. Two distinguished scientists who are also convinced Christians tried to persuade me to do just that. John Polkinghorne argued that a Divine Creator was as good an explanation as any other for the fact that the universe is fine-tuned for the development of conscious life and Simon Conway Morris argued that if there is an element of 'directionality' in evolution, that would be an 'intellectually coherent argument' for keeping an open mind on whether there is a creative intelligence behind the universe.

I am not a scientist, so on what authority do I reject these arguments? My answer is that whether or not there is a God is not a scientific question. However tempting it is to argue from the structure of the universe to the existence of God, there is no logical connection between the two, between our scientific knowledge of the material world and our philosophical speculation about the meaning of our existence. As Martin Rees told me at the start of my journey, 'the pre-eminent mystery of why anything exists at all is beyond science.' This does not stop scientists who are Christians trying to make the connection. John Polkinghorne even suggests that there is a hint of an anti-Copernican revolution in a universe that is hospitable to intelligent life on our planet. Perhaps we are at the centre of God's creation after all.

My admiration for John Polkinghorne is genuine – he is the Marshal Ney of the Christian retreat from superstition – but neither his reasoned argument nor Simon Conway Morris's had any impact on my scepticism. However eerily well-constructed the universe turns out to be, it can never be an argument for the existence of God.

At the risk of sounding pretentious, I call Ludwig Wittgenstein as a witness. Ever since Don Cupitt made me feel like an undergraduate who had failed to read the recommended texts, I have been dipping into the philosophers he assumed I had read, and I am struck by what Wittgenstein has to say on this question of whether science can throw any light on the mystery of why anything exists at all. 'Not <u>how</u> the world is, is the mystical, but <u>that</u> it is,' he writes. He goes on to explain that how the world is is a scientific matter with scientific answers but we are still left with what he calls the 'thatness' of the world, the fact that it is. He concludes, 'We feel that even if <u>all possible</u> scientific questions be answered, the problems of life have not been touched at all.' In other words, the 'thatness' of the world is beyond science.

If the reasoned arguments for the existence of a Creator God put forward by scientists are flawed, as I believe they are, I am left with the one reasoned argument that really caught my imagination. Timothy Radcliffe recognises that science cannot throw any light on the pre-eminent mystery. Science helps us to understand the world but not to make sense of it and it is this 'making sense of it' that is the key to his use of the word God. What makes sense of human existence, he believes, is our capacity for unpossessive love. If we were not capable of this form of selflessness, then life would indeed be a tale told by an idiot signifying nothing. When he speaks of God, he is not speaking of a person whose existence can be proved or disproved and whose fingerprints on the universe can be identified by scientists desperately seeking a Creator. He is speaking of an awakening to the possibility that human existence has a meaning, a significance beyond itself. So he says, 'What gives meaning, what makes sense of our lives? For human beings throughout history the capacity for unpossessive love gives at least a glimpse of what our lives may be about.'

Timothy opened my eyes to something that has no doubt been obvious to most people since the time of Confucius and that is that the significant and hopeful fact about humanity is our capacity for acting with a degree of selflessness that Timothy calls unpossessive love. What I do not understand is how Timothy makes the connection between this hopeful human characteristic and the idea of God. He is not, I think, suggesting that God programmed evolution to produce this effect or intervened in the process to give evolution this unDarwinian twist. But he is suggesting that the unDarwinian twist should at least make me stop and think about the possibility that human existence has some meaning beyond itself.

If we have reached a stage of evolution where we are capable of overruling our selfish drives so much the better but I do not understand in what sense this gives meaning to human existence. As individuals we can give our lives a meaning, though we probably express it as a purpose or an ambition, and the human community can identify a goal such as the eradication of child poverty but this is not what Timothy is talking about. He is talking about our existence on this speck in the universe having a meaning and significance we have not given it, and that is where he loses me. Who else is there other than ourselves to give meaning and significance to our lives? I can accept that for human beings throughout history the capacity for selflessness has been something to cherish, to give us hope that we are not just wild animals with a veneer of civilisation but I cannot accept that this singular human attribute is a reason to believe that human existence has a meaning beyond itself. As I realised all too clearly when I was talking with Sister Maria Boulding, 'beyond' is somewhere I cannot go, a country I do not recognise.

Timothy Radcliffe's God really did catch my imagination so that I feel like a man who knows he has turned down the best offer he is likely to get. I wish I could share Timothy's confidence that our lives are about something, that we are not the casual and meaningless product of evolution but I cannot; and the irony is that it is my encounter with the intelligent, sincere faith of Christians such as Timothy Radcliffe and Sister Maria Boulding that has encouraged me to be honest about my own position. When you turn down a faith you wish you could share not because you are uncertain but because you are sure that human life has no meaning beyond itself, it is time to stop calling yourself an agnostic.

David: " Is this the real `thought motivation' as to why JR is not prepared to take a step into the unknown (unknowable)

My nonbelief was pretty well ingrained at the beginning of my journey but what tilted agnosticism towards atheism was something Martin Rees told me last summer about the death throes of the sun. I remember sitting in the cool of Trinity College Chapel and wondering why I had never realised that life on planet earth would one day be extinguished forever. The almost impossible to grasp length of time between now and then does not alter the fact that we are heading for oblivion. If that is the case, doesn't it make better sense to accept the truth that stares us in the face – the human adventure had a beginning and will have an end and that is all there is to it – rather than to go on looking for a meaning that is not there?

Once I had started to think seriously about atheism, that process was given impetus by my meetings with Richard Dawkins and Julian Baggini, Julian's distinction between dogmatic and undogmatic atheism making me question for the first time whether agnosticism was a tenable position. Even so, I was reluctant to abandon agnosticism. Atheism would be a firm commitment and that went against the grain of my character. Keeping my options open and hedging my bets was more my style. I had felt entirely at home with the agnosticism of Martin Rees and Andrew Huxley and when I was in Edinburgh with Richard Holloway, I thought I would happily settle for his defiant brand of 'committed unknowing'. Even Don Cupitt's non-realist interpretation of Christian doctrine, or Christianity with the supernatural taken out, seemed preferable to slamming the door on Christianity altogether.

That unwillingness to slam the door on people whose faith I had admired and believed to be genuine, and with whose personality I had felt an immediate rapport, was more than anything else what stood between me and atheism. Yet, I realised, of course, that dishonesty about my own position would be no basis for continuing a dialogue with believers.

Somewhere along my journey, the last few traces of belief that I had retained from childhood disappeared like the morning mist and the main features of my nonbelief became clear. In relation to the pre-eminent mystery of why anything exists at all, I am still an agnostic but on the question of whether God is the solution to that mystery I am an atheist. I am as sure as it is possible to be that any God we propose as the solution to the pre-eminent mystery is a product of our own imagination. There is no other God, no other reality, no meaning to human existence that we have not thought up for ourselves. I shall call myself an undogmatic atheist, not because I think there is an outside chance that there is a God after all, but because I want to distance myself from militant atheism. I remain strongly opposed to the mockery of religion I witnessed at Conway Hall and, like Lewis Wolpert, I have no wish to persuade other people to abandon their beliefs.

What difference will being an undogmatic atheist make? I am glad I do not entertain false hopes of a life after death or believe that this life has a meaning beyond itself. Knowing that this is the only life I shall ever have makes me appreciate all the more how fortunate I am to have been given the chance to take part in the human adventure and how foolish it would be not to cherish relationships that will never come again; and knowing that life has no meaning beyond itself, makes me realise that whatever is going to be good about the future of humanity depends on us alone. Being an atheist also re-enforces my belief that every human life is precious. We are not incarnations of the divine but each one of us is unique and will never have another chance. I believe human existence is meaningless but I do not believe it is worthless.

I shall continue to attend church services from time to time because I enjoy ritual and a good sing. Like Martin Rees I am still a parasite on religion. But I shall not be joining one of those societies that cater for nonbelievers. My contacts with them suggest that they like to see themselves as a minority in an overwhelmingly believing society and I do not think they are anything of the sort. My guess is that whatever people say in response to surveys, the majority in this country are nonbelievers. They will not call themselves atheists because that sensible English hypocrisy prevents them but I suspect

David questions this — a lot of people have a sense of 'spirit' or spiritual presence

that most people are, like me, agnostics on the mystery of why anything exists at all and undogmatic atheists on the question of God.

I could have predicted that this would be my destination but I could not have forseen that the journey that has led me to undogmatic atheism would also give me an optimism about the future that I did not have before. The explanation for this apparent contradiction lies in the unanimity with which so many of those I met, whether they were believers or agnostics or atheists, agreed that what was hopeful about the future of humanity was that we are capable of rebelling against our innate selfishness. People who would never have agreed on the question of God, nevertheless agree on the significance of this singular human characteristic. The convinced Christian, Timothy Radcliffe calls it a capacity for 'unpossessive love.' The convinced atheist, Richard Dawkins, calls it 'unDarwinian selflessness.' The Anglican bishop, David Stancliffe, calls it 'love in which we seek nothing for ourselves.' For Don Cupitt, it is 'disinterested morality' and for Karen Armstrong it is 'practical compassion' which she defines as 'the capacity to dethrone ourselves from the centre of the world and put others there.' This singular human characteristic is commonly called altruism but I much prefer the more expressive terms used by Radclliffe and Dawkins – unpossessive love and unDarwinian selflessness.

According to Karen Armstrong, the idea that humanity's best hope is to cultivate our capacity for selflessness is as old as the hills so it is not surprising that it should have cropped up so often on my journey. What is surprising and what makes me not just an undogmatic atheist but an optimistic one, is that the significance of this singular human capacity was urged upon me by both believers and nonbelievers. I am thinking particularly of my meetings with Timothy Radcliffe and Richard Dawkins, near-neighbours and complete strangers who represent the opposite poles of belief and nonbelief, and yet who share a conviction that humanity's best hope lies in our capacity for selflessness. Together, these two men provide the answer to Umberto Eco's question. Yes, there is a notion of hope (and of our responsibility to the future) that can be shared by believers and nonbelievers; and it can be based on the one human characteristic that gives us a reason to hope, our ability to overrule our innate selfishness. Where that ability comes from, what is required to ensure its survival and what role religion plays, are questions on which believers and nonbelievers may disagree but they share the same hope nevertheless.

When I try to think of examples of unDarwinian selflessness, it is the exceptional cases that come to mind. John Polkinghorne told me the true story of a father who offered to donate his second kidney to his son when the first kidney transplant had failed. More widely known is the example of Father Maximilien Kolbe, a Polish priest who persuaded the guards in a concentration camp to let him be executed in place of a man who had a wife and children. The family man survived and attended the canonisation of St. Maximilien Kolbe in 1982. Such exceptional cases were clearly on the mind of Cardinal Martini when he replied to Umberto Eco's question. He gave this illustration of what believers and nonbelievers would recognise as hopeful about human nature.

'This is particularly apparent when we see someone who, in the pursuit of higher values, puts himself willingly in harm's way, even when there is no promise of reward.'

But exceptional cases, however striking as illustrations of selflessness, are not, I think, what those I met had in mind. When Timothy Radcliffe spoke of unpossessive love or Karen Armstrong defined compassion as the capacity to dethrone ourselves from the centre of the world and put others there, they were talking about a fundamental change in the way we relate to other people. Either way – extraordinary acts of selflessness or fundamental change in our attitude to other people – everyone I met seems to agree that we all have this capacity for selflessness whether we use it or not.

Richard Dawkins explanation of how this capacity developed is well known. We have evolved what he calls 'conscious foresight' – our ability to simulate the future in imagination – and it is this that enables us to defy our fundamental selfishness. Altruism may or may not be built into our human nature, he says, but we can see the benefits of cultivating and nurturing altruism, 'something that has no place in nature, something that has never existed before in the whole history of the world.' But for the Christians I met, evolution is not an adequate explanation. Our capacity for selflessness, unprecedented in four billion years of evolution, is interpreted by some Christians as a hint of the divine presence in the Universe and by others as the one thing that makes sense of and gives meaning to our lives.

I do not think it matters what we believe about the origin of our capacity for selflessness as long as we recognise its special significance for the future of humanity. I do not think it matters what we believe about God as long as we agree that the best hope for humanity is to cultivate and nurture this singular human capacity. It will need cultivating. When I asked Andrew Huxley how he thought evolution would develop, he said it was possible that our less attractive characteristics, our selfishness and aggression, would be the ones to survive. Our fundamental selfishness is not going to wither away.

If religion helps to nurture our selflessness, I am all for it, though I shall never be religious myself. If religion hinders the growth of selflessness, I am all against it. My atheism does not set me against religion. It sets me against the sort of religion that divides people into the damned and the elect, that encourages intolerance and bigotry rather than selflessness and empathy with others. I agree wholeheartedly with Karen Armstrong. If your belief makes you kind and respectful of others, it is good religion; if it makes you belligerent and intolerant, it is not good religion, however firm your belief. I do not agree with Peter Atkins that religion is a malign force in the world. History provides (and continues to provide) plenty of evidence that religion can bring out the worst in men but there is plenty of evidence, too, that religion has helped to nurture our capacity for selflessness. Sheltering from the rain in St. Peter's Square and reflecting on the resilience of Christianity, I thought that death was religion's trump card but I was wrong. Religion's trump card is our fundamental selfishness and a long as religion helps to curb that side of our nature and to encourage our capacity for selflessness, I see no reason why an undogmatic atheist should not regard religion as an ally. We share the same hope, don't we?

I am not trying to persuade myself that there is no difference between belief and atheism, nor have I forgotten that Christian hope is not the same as human optimism. I am just trying to explain that despite the fundamental difference between Timothy Radcliffe's conviction that our lives make sense and have meaning and my conviction that we are the casual and meaningless product of evolution, there is still room for a shared hope. Of Christian hope, Timothy wrote this: 'Because of the child whose birth we celebrate with each passing year, we can say "humanity has a future."' To which I respond that nonbelievers, too, can say that "humanity has a future" but our hope springs from the singular human capacity for selflessness, of which, Jesus, the child-grown-up was a supreme example.

That is the end of the journey. When I set out I called myself an agnostic. I now know that I am an undogmatic atheist. It is a destination but I doubt whether it is the end of my travels. There are too many questions still unanswered. I am at home in my undogmatic atheism but my new-found optimism depends on believers and non-believers sharing the same hope for the future, based on the singular human capacity for selflessness. That sounds fine in theory but what do I really know about this singular human capacity? Supposing Timothy Radcliffe and Richard Dawkins are wrong and there is no such thing as unpossessive love or unDarwinian selflessness, and that the cynics are right when they say that no one acts selflessly unless there is a reward in this life or the next?

Once I start thinking along these lines, other questions suggest themselves but the question that, more than any other, convinces me that my travels are not over is the one that is bound to interest me most now that I am an undogmatic atheist. 'Is it possible to overrule our fundamental selfishness without the help of a religious faith?' Sister Maria Boulding was adamant that only by making ourselves a conduit for God's love are we capable of overruling our innate selfishness. Writing to Umberto Eco, Cardinal Martini said he found it difficult to see how altruism could be sustained unless its absolute value was founded on metaphysical principles or on a personal God. And Dr Rowan Williams, in his criticism of Don Cupitt's idea that religion is a useful myth to support a disinterested morality, asks how disinterestedness can make sense 'without a focus <u>beyond</u> our present self-consciousness.' Or in plain English: 'Can we be good without God?'

Naturally, I think we can and that an atheist can nurture selflessness as well as a believer but I have no evidence that this is true and I am not sure where the evidence could be found. Perhaps I should trawl through history and the contemporary world looking for examples of unpossessive love and unDarwinian selflessness to see what sort of people they are who have freed themselves from being the centre of the universe or who, in the pursuit of higher values, have put themselves willingly in harm's way, even when there is no promise of reward. And as I turn this idea over in my mind, Jack Mahoney's words come back to me: 'you will probably find that as one journey ends another begins.'

Lightning Source UK Ltd.
Milton Keynes UK
UKHW011424260419
341672UK00005B/1005/P